PARENTING
Without
DISTRACTION

The Attunetion® Approach

ISBN: 0615703607
ISBN 13: 9780615703602
Library of Congress Control Number: 2012917871
The Attunetion® Approach, Albuquerque, NM

DEDICATION

This book is dedicated to Betty, whose loving and
attuned friendship has been an
inspiration for me since I was ten years old. Thank you
for all you've been for me.

And

To my family: my wife, Susan, our son, Kevin, and
his wife Amy. I cherish your
endless support and unconditional love. You are
my constant reminder of what matters
most and how paying Attunetion enriches our lives.

Acknowledgments

Behind anyone's dream fulfilled, vision realized, or the completion of any meaningful accomplishment stands a team that made it all possible. I am so blessed to have such a team, and I am so deeply grateful for them.

I want to thank my writer, Carole Jacobs, a great friend and partner who inspired and authored this book. You have my endless gratitude, for without you this book would not be possible.

My Attunetion team: Nathan Hoge and Courtney Custer. You both have been so dedicated to this work, believing in me, and believing in the mission of the Attunetion work. I am so grateful for your standing by me and that work, even through the long days when it looked like it all might never happen. Thank you for your steadfast support, inspiration, and incredible talent.

I am also so appreciative of those dedicated people at Southwest Family Guidance Center and Institute: Rick Hunt, Mary Jepsen, and Raana Azad for keeping the operation going in my absence and working on this project, to the supervisors who have stepped in and provided such great leadership and direction, and to all the therapists and staff who every day tune in to what matters most to the families we serve.

Contents

INTRODUCTION:

It's All About Connection

Sometimes inspiration comes when it's least expected.

It was the end of a long day. Before I could finally head home, I had one more commitment: a conference call with a team of coaches I had hired to help me prepare for an upcoming presentation. Carole, Pam, and I had worked together before, so they already knew how I felt about the high cost of distracted parenting and its impact on society.

"Good afternoon, ladies. How are you today?"

"We're good, Craig. How 'bout you—how was your day?"

"It was an especially tough one. Seven suicide assessments. One especially heartbreaking case of bullying in the schools. Kids in trauma and in trouble. We're seeing more and more of this."

"Why do you think this is happening—I mean, why are so many kids at risk?"

"That's a good question, Carole. Bottom line: parents are so distracted these days by everything that's going on in their lives that they've lost sight of what matters most—and that's their relationships with their kids. If only we could get them to pay Attunetion."

"Craig, did you just say 'Attunetion'?"

"Sorry, I meant to say 'attention.' Parents need to pay better attention to what's going on in their children's lives."

"Hang on a sec—I think Attunetion is actually the perfect word. To have a healthy relationship with your child, you need to pay attention and tune in. You need both, don't you?"

"You do. Good parenting is all about making healthy connections with your kids. But unless you're paying attention and tuning in to the right thing, at the right time and in the right way, that vital connection won't happen."

"Craig, I think you need to share your Attunetion Approach. It's a simple but powerful strategy that any parents can use to raise their children with more ease, confidence, and love."

And that's how **Parenting without Distraction: The Attunetion® Approach** came to be.

I wrote this book with the simple premise that no one knows your kids and what they need better than you do.

Parenting without Distraction: The Attunetion Approach provides a simple framework, based on sound parameters, that any parent can use. It suggests that kids need love, boundaries, and consistency. It also suggests that parents need to take greater responsibility for the way they raise their children. But within these broad parameters, the Attunetion Approach recognizes that there are many ways to raise your kids that result in good outcomes for everyone.

The Attunetion Approach is based on tuning in to what's important to you and your family, and then using three simple steps to create that within your family. In other words, to raise happy, healthy, responsible children, you need to pay attention and tune in to the right thing, at the right time and in the right way, for you and your kids. It's that simple.

The Attunetion Approach works because if you can do all three—if you can pay attention and tune in to the right thing, at the right time and in the right way, you can create more positive relationships at home, at work, and in every corner of your life.

If you are as concerned about the health and well-being of our kids as I am, this book is for you. Because whether you're a parent, an educator, a health-care professional, or simply someone who is feeling unconnected in today's high-stress world, there is true and lasting value in paying Attunetion.

NOTES

CHAPTER 1:

The Power of Attunetion®

When was the last time someone gave you his or her full and undivided attention? Didn't it feel great to be noticed…to be seen…to be valued?

As human beings, we're wired for connection. In fact, from the moment of birth, our very survival depends on it.

At each developmental stage, an infant must have a close attachment with a consistent caregiver to ensure safety and protection. This first loving experience not only affects a child's long-term emotional welfare; each experience also builds new neural pathways, the basic building blocks of the brain.

For example, when a mother responds to her baby's cry of hunger quickly and consistently, the child learns to trust that her needs will be met and that her relationship with her mother is safe and secure. But what if the mother ignores her baby's cry of hunger? A different pathway of connection is made; in this instance, the child may learn that crying may or may not get her what she needs.

Not surprisingly, the parent-child bond is the primary force in your child's social, emotional, intellectual, and physical development. It provides a solid foundation for a child's sense of security and well-being. It teaches your child that he is loved and valued. It's what calms your child during times of stress, and it's what will give her confidence to take risks and grow.

Children who feel the most secure in their early relationships with parents have tremendous advantages in life. They tend to grow up with good self-esteem. They cope well with life's ups and downs, and they have a strong capacity for empathy. These kids naturally form other healthy, close relationships as they go out into the world.

Contrast this with children whose parent-child bonds aren't as strong.

They tend to grow up feeling more insecure and needy. They often lack self-control and have trouble dealing with stress and adversity. They experience challenges when it comes to making and maintaining friendships. And they often have difficulty with trust, intimacy, and affection. All too often, these kids are misdiagnosed with attention deficit disorder (ADD), bipolar disorder, and other mental-health issues, when in reality their lack of impulse control and inability to self-regulate are a direct result of impaired brain development stemming from insecure parent-child bonds. This feeling of disconnection can lead to other, more serious problems as well, such as difficulty learning, mental-health issues such as depression, and susceptibility to chronic illness, substance abuse, anger problems, promiscuity, early pregnancy, and criminal behavior.

So why do some children form secure attachments while others not so much?

There are lots of reasons some parent-child bonds are less strong than others. Sometimes parents themselves are facing profound issues such as anxiety and depression, substance abuse, or trauma that make it difficult for them to connect with their kids. Sometimes it's the child who faces an obstacle that stands in the way of forming a secure attachment—for example, a child with a difficult temperament or developmental issue that makes it hard for his or her parents to connect with him emotionally or physically. Other times, parents are so preoccupied coping with the stress of daily life that they're unable to tune in to their children's feelings and needs. Whatever the reason, a failure to connect can have a significant and lasting impact on a child's emotional development and growth.

Fortunately, most parents don't face such difficult hurdles. However, sometimes the parent-child bond is threatened not by a major life crisis but by something as simple as distracted living.

Distracted living is chipping away at the quality of our relationships with our kids, our partners, and each other. In fact, today's fast-paced, hectic world is edging out our ability to be fully present parents, and it's seeping into our relationships with our children. More and more, you see otherwise good parents "checking out" because they are trying to do too much—the mom who is squeezing in "just" one more errand even though her toddler is wailing with exhaustion; the parents who are watching TV while only half-listening as their child tries to tell them about a difficult day at school; or the dad who is busy texting a friend and misses the goal his son makes at his varsity soccer match.

Tuning out a child on occasion is understandable. However, when parents consistently ignore or miss opportunities to connect, they set in motion an unintended spiral of negative attention and challenging behaviors—behaviors that will carry forward, impacting not only the child's ability to fulfill his potential, but also how he will connect with others in the future.

Fortunately, there's an antidote for distracted parenting…and it's called the Attunetion Approach.

The Attunetion Approach means paying attention and tuning in to the right thing, at the right time and in the right way, for you and your child. Because when you can do all three—when you pay attention and tune in to the right thing, at the right time and in the right way, it sets the stage for stronger connections to occur.

Just as a climbing rose bush needs a lattice on which to grow, your children need you to provide footholds to help them develop physically and emotionally. For this to occur, you need to pay Attunetion. In other words, you need to put your attention and focus on what matters most: your kids.

To understand why, consider how the Attunetion Approach can help you become a more responsive parent to a newborn.

- **Pay attention to the right thing.** Understanding what your baby needs or wants can be difficult at first. However, the more you pay attention, the more you learn what each of your child's sounds, movements, and expressions means. For example, your baby may use a high-pitched wail when he's hungry and a much lower-pitched, short cry when he's tired. By paying Attunetion to the circumstances and pattern of your child's cry, you can quickly learn to identify one from the other.

- **Pay attention to the right thing at the right time.** Hunger is often the cause of distress in babies. Maintaining a feeding schedule can be helpful in keeping your child calm and happy; however, pay attention to the right thing at the right time. Your baby's sudden fussiness or prolonged crying may be a signal that she is hitting a growth spurt or other developmental change and requires more time feeding or cuddling.

- **Pay attention to the right thing, at the right time and in the right way.** Talking, facial expressions, and gestures are as important to a baby's development as food or sleep. Pay Attunetion the next time you are feeding or diapering your child. Are you talking and playing with your baby while also tending to his needs? Are you speaking to your child with a calm and even tone of voice? The way you interact with your child builds trust and teaches him to feel safe and secure. In contrast, if you take the position that newborns need little more than

> **Tuning In**
>
> "Attunetion" means paying attention and tuning in to the right thing, at the right time and in the right way for you and your child. Because if you can do all three—if you can pay attention and tune in to the right thing, at the right time and in the right way, you can create more positive relationships at home, at work, and in every corner of your life.

feeding and diaper changes, you may miss an important opportunity to connect.

Don't worry if you don't always "read" your baby on the first try. The parent-child bond is amazingly strong and resilient. As long as you pay Attunetion and notice when you've missed your child's cue and then continue to try to figure out what he or she needs, the process of building the parent-child bond will continue on track.

Paying Attunetion to the right thing, at the right time and in the right way for you and your child, helps you recognize what your child is feeling and thinking and what he or she needs. When you pay Attunetion, your child senses your interest and approval. This, in turn, helps deepen the level of connection between you and your child.

Right thing. Right time. Right way. That's the power of Attunetion Parenting.

Making the Connection

What are some of the signs of a secure versus insecure attachment?

Secure Parent-Child Bond	Insecure Parent-Child Bond
Maintains emotional balance	Lacks self-control
Shows confidence in him/herself	Demonstrates low self-esteem
Shares feelings and seeks support	Lacks empathy, compassion, and remorse
Demonstrates independence	Tends to be needy and/or clingy
Often performs well in school	Experiences behavioral and academic problems at school
Rebounds from disappointment and loss	Inability to deal with stress and adversity
Connects with others in a healthy way	Has difficulty with trust, intimacy, and affection
Has well-regulated emotions and behaviors	Inability to self-regulate emotions; poor impulse control

Think on This

"Each day of our lives we make deposits in the memory banks of our children."

—*Charles R. Swindoll*

Catch and Connect: Heading Off Tantrums

Have you ever gotten "the look" from others when your child acted out in public...when your child threw herself down on the floor of the cereal aisle, wailing at the top of her lungs, *"But I want Fruity Os!"*?

One young mom expressed her frustration at this all-too-common situation:

> *It seems like every time we take Ashley out to dinner with us, she throws a fit the minute we put her in the highchair. She kicks. She screams. She throws the silverware on the floor. It's awful. If I take her out of the chair and into the bathroom, I'm just spoiling her by giving in. If I leave her in the chair and pretend not to notice, the people seated around us get annoyed. I feel like we can't win.*

As every parent can painfully attest, there is nothing that can bring you to your knees faster than a toddler having a tantrum. When you have a child who consistently acts out, dining out isn't fun; travel isn't fun; even a simple trip to the grocery can be exhausting.

Rather than getting into a power struggle with your child or stressing out about what other people think, focus instead on what you can do to Catch and Connect.

To Catch, first understand what's driving the behavior.

Most toddlers don't set out to make their parents miserable or to put on a "show." Toddlers throw tantrums because they don't yet have the skills needed to self-regulate—in other words, to manage their own needs and feelings. Pay attention and tune in to what your child is trying to tell you. Is your child tired? Hungry? Over-stimulated? Bored or frustrated? Very often tantrums occur because your toddler is trying to communicate a feeling or a need and is frustrated over not being understood.

Once you identify the triggers, Connect the steps that can help you avoid and/or deal with a tantrum situation.

- Schedule your activities around your child's peak times, and avoid putting added stress on your child when she's likely to be tired, hungry, or over-stimulated.

- Bring along snacks, drinks, and a new or favorite toy to keep your toddler distracted and occupied.

- Praise good behavior, and be clear about how you will deal with bad behavior should it occur. A toddler is not too young to understand the consequences of his behavior.

- Hold your child accountable if a tantrum occurs—even if it means leaving the grocery store before you're finished shopping.

- Maintain your cool when your child acts out; yelling will only serve to escalate your child's distress. Instead, model calm, loving behavior that helps your child learn that her needs can be met without making a fuss.

Bottom Line: Your child won't have tantrums forever. As he develops and improves his ability to make his needs known, the tantrums will diminish.

What Comes Next

Maybe you "lost it" at your children because they interrupted while you were answering email from home. Perhaps you berated your son because his report card wasn't what you expected. Or maybe you brushed off your daughter's request to watch a movie together so that you could fold laundry or pay the bills.

There are times when parenting doesn't go as planned; when you're so stressed out or tired that you make choices that aren't ideal.

Take a deep breath and cut yourself some slack. There is no such thing as a perfect parent. We all make mistakes and we all fall short sometimes when it comes to raising our kids. But here's what matters most: that you take responsibility for your words and actions and that you hold yourself accountable for making things right with your kids. In other words, you Catch and Connect to reestablish the vital bond you have with your children.

So how do you know how to Catch and Connect?

Here, and at the end of each subsequent chapter, you'll find a series of exercises designed to help you pay attention and tune in to what you and your children need most.

As you engage in these exercises, you'll need a place to keep your notes. Whether you use the pages at the end of each chapter, or dedicate a special journal, a simple pad of paper or a folder on your computer dedicated to taking notes, it's important to record the date as well as your thoughts, insights and what you learn along the way. By putting the date on each entry, you can keep track of progress and setbacks. Over time, those insights may help you tune into those things that can help you parent with greater confidence, ease and love.

Your Turn

"Because I SAID SO!" "Go to your room, NOW!" "Just wait till your father gets home." Have you ever found yourself saying something to your children you swore you'd never say and then afterwards, you ask yourself: "Where did THAT come from?" Then it hits you: you sound just like your mother and father.

Like it or not, a lot of what we say and do is ingrained in us from our own childhoods. This can be a good thing, especially when we take on characteristics that we respect and admire. But what about those influences that can make parenting harder than it needs to be? To be the best mom or dad for your kids, focus on the 3 A's of Attunetion Parenting: **Attitude, Accountability** and **Action**.

1. **Attitude.** As a parent, you get to decide which parenting techniques and values you want to incorporate into your family life—and which ones you don't. To differentiate between the two, jot down your thoughts below or in your journal as you think about the following questions:

What are you biggest struggles and frustrations as a parent?

As you reflect on this question, pay attention to your own attitudes and reactions. For example, do you routinely lose patience when trying to get your little ones to bed at night? Do you snap at your kids when they start bickering in the backseat during afterschool pickup? Do you find you make sarcastic or berating comments about your teenager's appearance?

The attitude you lead with sets the stage for how your children will respond and react. For example, let's say your toddler has recently taken to saying "No!" each time you try to help him get ready for daycare. If your attitude is positive ("My child is developing a healthy sense of independence."), you're more likely to react to your son's behavior in a positive way. Thus, by showing him patience and affection, your son will learn that it's natural and okay for him to demonstrate greater independence as he gets older.

In contrast, if your attitude about his behavior is negative, you're more likely to respond in a negative, punishing way ("You're going into time out if you don't hurry up and let me help."). When a child feels threatened or unloved because of a parent's negative attitude, he is more likely to develop negative feelings about himself, which ultimately leads to even more challenging behavior.

Take a moment and think of a recent situation where you lost patience with your child. What could you do differently next time to help your child to a more positive outcome?

2. **Accountability.** One of the best ways to stop negative thinking is for you to first recognize it in yourself and to hold yourself accountable for what comes next—in other words, to pay attention and tune in to your own attitudes about your children and to take responsibility for how you express those feelings. For many of us, that means taking a look back at how we were parented.

Make a list of what your parents did that helped you become the person you are today. Did your parents make you feel confident and secure? Were they encouraging? Empowering?

Next, take a few moments and jot down the ways in which you disagree with their parenting style. For example, are there any ways they disciplined you that you feel are inappropriate for *your* children? Were they less encouraging than you felt you needed? In what way? Did their actions lead you to question your own abilities as you grew?

The purpose here isn't to point fingers; it's to remind you that when it comes to your own family, you are accountable for the decisions you make. And that means you get to pick and choose to adopt the best of your parent's parenting skills and to gently discard those attitudes and traits that don't work for you and your children.

3. **Action.** As a parent, you are THE biggest influence shaping your children's lives. Turning in to your own behavior, and holding yourself accountable for your attitudes and your actions is a big part of helping them to develop healthy self-esteem and habits.

    Think about a time recently when your child came to you with a problem. How did you handle the situation?

    Now ask yourself: What impact did your response have on your child? How might your child feel empowered by your response or belittled by it?

If the outcome wasn't as positive as you would have liked, what could you do next time to better Catch and Connect with your child?

By making the connection between actions and outcomes, you may gain important insight on what it means to pay attention to the right thing, at the right time and in the right way for you and your child.

Think on This

> "Your attitude determines how
> you experience the world."
>
> —*Sanaya Roman*

NOTES

CHAPTER 2:

The Gift of YOU

For most parents today, time is an issue—a BIG issue.

Between work, household chores and upkeep, cooking, shopping, laundry, and other tasks, there simply aren't enough hours in the day to get everything done. And, of course, you also need to take care of your kids.

The thing about children is that they consume a lot of time. Time to get them cleaned, dressed, fed, and ready for school. Time to pick them up in the afternoon, shuttle them to their activities, feed them, help with homework, and get them ready for bed.

And that's assuming everything goes as planned.

If there are problems at school or at home, you have to deal with them as well. Somewhere, you also need time for yourself—to catch up on email, to watch your favorite show, to connect with friends and family. No wonder so many parents feel overwhelmed and stressed.

But what about the impact of distraction on your children? How are *they* coping with the frantic pace of daily life?

Distracted parenting creates an unintended spiral of emotional and behavioral issues. Consider this all-too-typical example:

- **Child (pulling on her parent's sleeve):** I want it!

- **Parent (texting a friend):** No.

- **Child (louder):** I want it!!

- **Parent (still texting):** No.

- **Child (now jumping up and down and screaming):** I want it!!!!

- **Parent (finally looking at child):** Okay, but you have to stop whining.

When parents aren't paying Attunetion—when they aren't tuning in to the right thing, at the right time and in the right way, they very often end up creating the kind of behaviors they want to avoid with their kids.

When parents aren't physically and emotionally present, children feel a sense of disconnection and loss. Depending on the level of distraction in the home, they may even feel emotionally abandoned and/or rejected. If this goes on long enough, they may come to see themselves as undeserving, unloved, and unimportant.

Some kids, like the child in our example, act out and regress to behaviors they long grew out of. Others become aloof or angry and pretend to be unaffected. The more stressed and distracted we become, the more our children challenge us and the more difficult it is to get them under control.

- The two-year-old rolling on the floor, kicking, screaming, and biting? That's a child calling out for Attunetion.

- The five-year-old who has become clingy, demanding that you lie down with her at night and read endless stories? That's a child calling out for Attunetion.

- The ten-year-old who suddenly is getting into fights at school? That's a child calling out for Attunetion.

- The fifteen-year-old who, once cheerful, now hides in his room playing video games instead of doing his homework? That's a child calling out for Attunetion.

- The twenty-year-old on scholarship who comes home from college with a failing report card and bright purple hair? That's a child calling out for Attunetion.

Children need to know they are being seen and heard. And, typically, they will seek the attention they need one way or another, even if it means acting out. Negative patterns of behavior may simply be their way to express their distress the only way they know how. As a parent, it's up to you to pay Attunetion—to acknowledge their feelings and to take proper steps to address them.

The more available and emotionally attuned you are as a parent—that is, the more you pay Attunetion and tune in to the right thing, at the right time and in the right way for your kids, the more connected your children will feel and the more likely they'll be to cooperate.

- Let's say you're a new parent. Paying Attunetion means tuning in to your baby's cries so that you can tell if he is hungry, tired, needing a diaper change, or wanting a cuddle.

- Let's say your child is now three years old. Paying Attunetion means tuning in to your toddler's growing impatience as he plays so that you know if your son needs quiet time, a snack, or a change of activity.

- Let's say your child is now thirteen. Paying Attunetion means tuning in to your daughter's shifting food preferences so you can tell if she may be adopting healthier eating habits, expressing her views about animal rights, or struggling with issues of self-image and weight.

- And let's say your child is now six feet tall and eighteen years old. Paying Attunetion to the right thing means tuning in so that you can tell if your son's sudden interest in body piercings suggests he may be exploring his individuality, following a fad, or falling into other, more dangerous habits and behaviors.

Attunetion prompts you to take a closer look at the feelings behind your child's actions so that you can determine which things are most important and which ones can be dealt with later, or maybe not at all. It can help you sort through the issues of daily living so you can be the best parent for your child.

Where to begin?

- **Pay attention to the right thing.** Notice how your child expresses his or her emotions. Whether your child is happy or sad, eager or frustrated, loving or angry, it's important to acknowledge your child's feelings. Doing so can help your child to better understand his or her emotions and learn to manage them in a positive way.

- **Pay attention to the right thing at the right time.** Take advantage of daily routines in order to be more present in your child's life. Meal, bath, and bed time all present wonderful opportunities to strengthen the vital connection between you and your child. By paying Attunetion at these routine parts of the day, you may find that, over time, your child is becoming less demanding because her needs for positive attention are already being met.

- **Pay attention to the right thing, at the right time and in the right way.** When was the last time you curled up on the couch and read with your six-year-old? Played catch with your twelve-year-old? Sat and watched a movie with your teenager? Each of these is an easy way to give your child Attunetion. Being present for your child doesn't always require a large commitment of time, however. A smile, a touch, sharing a knowing moment—each of these can communicate the love and pride you feel for your child.

The poet Walt Whitman said, *"When I give, I give myself."*

To look your children in the eye and tune in to what's really happening in their lives. To reflect what they're thinking and to be totally present with them. Isn't that what matters most in parenting?

Your children may whine that they want the toy hanging by the checkout line at the grocery, the latest sneakers or designer jeans, the iPad, or the car...but bottom line? It's *you* they want.

When you are fully present and engaged—in other words, when you're paying Attunetion to the right thing, at the right time and in the right way, you can have stronger connections and greater influence on your kids.

Tuning In

Slowing down for your children's emotions helps them to learn the lifelong skill of self-management—in other words, thinking before acting, and making good choices.

Making the Connection

Emotions of all kinds need to be noticed. The Attunetion Approach helps you create a loving place where your children can express themselves and share their important feelings.

- Start listening to your kids, even though they probably won't notice at first that you're tuning in to what's going on.

- Stop hurrying, and let your daughter finish her sentences, no matter how long or windy they may be.

- Give your son the opportunity to express himself without jumping in to correct him. Your presence as an active and loving listener is powerful stuff that can add confidence to your child's life.

- Avoid "yes/no" questions. Instead, encourage your children to talk more about things by asking open-ended questions. They can prompt discussion and open the door to new connections and deeper relationships.

Think on This

> "Too often we underestimate the power of a touch, a smile, a kind word, a listening ear, an honest compliment, or the smallest act of caring, all of which have the potential to turn a life around."
>
> —Leo Buscaglia

Catch and Connect: Putting the "Quality" into Quality Time

Picture this: it's lunchtime at a local sandwich shop.

Sitting at one table is a father and his young daughter. They're engrossed in conversation, coloring together as they wait for their meal to arrive. The child is animated and is happy to be spending time with her dad.

Seated across the room is another dad, also out for lunch with his little girl. As the pair wait for their food, the father is talking on his cell phone. The child sits quietly, looking increasingly bored and dejected.

Busy working lives and hectic schedules mean parents are increasingly running out of time to spend with their children. To make sure the precious time you have together counts, focus on what you can do to Catch and Connect.

To Catch, first recognize the impact your focused attention has on your children. Your Attunetion and approval are among the strongest rewards for kids. Telling your children that you love them isn't enough. Show them that you love them.

To Connect, spend ten minutes of quality time with each child every day. No excuses: you don't want to be the parent whose only "quality time" with his daughter was spent talking or texting on the phone while she sat waiting for your attention.

Turn off the cell phone and pay Attunetion. When you tune in to the right thing, at the right time and in the right way for your child, you're showing your child that she matters and, in doing so, you're building trust for the future.

Bottom Line: In the midst of our hectic schedules, we can sometimes forget how important it is to simply "be" with our kids. Yet giving our children our Attunetion is a vital part of healthy parent-child relationships.

Your Turn

A friend shared a story about parenting that underscores the power of Attunetion. It involved her frustration when, after putting her one-year old down for the night, he woke up screaming for attention. She went into his room, lifted him from his crib, and rocked him. Outwardly, it looked like the perfect picture of maternal love, but inside my friend felt her impatience growing as her mind flashed over the list of chores she had yet to attend to that night.

Come on Ben ... it's time for you to sleep. Hush now. Mommy has to clean up and do some laundry.

Ben continued to cry. It was then that this young mom tuned in and realized that her tone of voice and quick rocking motions weren't helping the situation. She took a deep breath, calmed herself and tuned in to what her son needed. As her voice became more soothing and her rocking motion slowed, Ben quickly quieted down and fell asleep.

This story is a simple one, but it proves an important point. Each and every day, our children demand we show up as parents. The attitudes we bring to this vital relationship has a profound impact on what happens next in our kids' development.

Take a moment and "become" your child. In other words, try to reflect from their eyes how they might be seeing you. Do they feel loved, seen, connected with you?

Think about the attributes you believe make for a good parent. List the top five.

1.

2.

3.

4.

Now think about this question from your child's perspective. If you asked your son or daughter to describe you, what would he or she say?

1.

2.

3.

4.

5.

Remember, when it comes to parenting, we have to be willing to be accountable. This doesn't mean we need to self-blame or judge; rather accountability empowers us to do our best each day, every day. But first, we have to be called to the possibility that our children will become what we model and expose them to.

Think on This

> "Each day you are leading by example. Whether you realize it or not or whether it's positive or negative, you are influencing those around you."
>
> —Rob Liano

Three Little Questions to Inspire Change

Our children exactly reflect our actions as well as our attitudes to parenting and to them. This means that if you want your children to be respectful and empathetic individuals, you need to treat them with respect and empathy. If you want them to be conscientious about their schoolwork, chores and other responsibilities, it's important to be conscientious in how you handle *your* responsibilities. And if you want your children to be healthy and happy in their lives, be healthy and happy in yours.

How can you help ensure that you're modeling the behavior you want your kids to reflect in their own lives? As you interact with your children, ask yourself:

1. What is your **attitude** (your tone of voice, your body language and facial expressions) telling your child about your intentions? For example, yelling at your upset daughter to calm down isn't going to help your child learn how to work her way through anger or frustration in the future.

2. What about your **actions**? If your goal is to teach your son about sportsmanship, calling out the ref when he rules against your son's team is actually modeling the exact opposite behavior you wanted your child to learn.

3. What happens when either your attitude and/or your actions don't match your intentions? Be **accountable**; Catch and Connect to turn things around:

   • Acknowledge that you didn't handle things the way you wanted.

   • Reflect your child's feelings.

   • Move forward – no one is perfect. What's important is that you stop and go back to repair the situation.

CHAPTER 3:

Love, Accountability, and Empathy

What are the three most important ingredients of a healthy parent-child relationship? Many experts believe they are:

- Love

- Accountability

- Empathy

Here's why.

Love as a way of living

From birth on, a child is dependent upon the physical and emotional care a parent provides. As you feed and bathe your baby, change diapers, and comfort and nurture him or her, your child builds an attachment to you. That attachment is the early seeds of love and sets the stage for the lifelong relationship between you and your child as well as your child's relationship with others.

A parent's love and caring determines how a child grows up and how that child will eventually parent. That love is so important that researchers sometimes call it the "super factor" of parenting. It is linked to better child behavior at all ages, and it provides children with a sense of security that helps them grow into confident and loving adults.

Accountability to build character

In contrast, holding kids accountable is one of the toughest parts of parenting. Many parents fail to make their children answer for poor decisions because they are afraid their kids will see them as being mean. As a result, they often excuse their kids for their bad choices, finding it easier to blame others, including themselves, when their children behave badly.

Setting limits and holding your child to them is how your child learns to function in the world. It's how your child gains the self-discipline necessary to manage her impulses and to behave in productive ways. It's also how your child develops an internal sense of right and wrong. By holding your child accountable for her actions and behaviors, and by being consistent and predictable in your responses, you're preparing her for an emotionally healthy, productive life.

Accountability offers an additional benefit: when your child learns to take responsibility for her actions and behaviors, family life becomes less strained, and that gives you more time to enjoy your child rather than policing her.

Empathy as a foundation for emotional health

The third component of a healthy parent-child relationship is **empathy**. Empathy is the ability to see things from another person's point of view and to respond in helpful, compassionate ways. It's a powerful force that allows us to coexist with others; it's what stops us from cruel or violent behavior, and it's what urges us to treat others with kindness.

When a parent shows empathy to a child, a deeper connection is formed. When you acknowledge your child's feelings, your child feels understood and valued. This not only strengthens the parent-child bond, it helps your child know that he or she isn't alone.

Empathy is like a mirror you hold up to your child. By acknowledging what he's experiencing, you help him to recognize and accept his own feelings—the first step in learning to cope with those feelings and helping them to lose their charge and dissipate. Without that mirror, children don't learn how to manage difficult emotions. Instead, feelings become repressed. And when feelings aren't acknowledged and dealt with, they pop out at unfortunate moments and in inappropriate ways, like when a toddler bites a playmate, a six-year-old develops a stutter, a ten-year-old starts to have recurring nightmares, or a teen develops a nervous tic.

So how do you raise emotionally healthy, empathetic kids? You already know: if you treat your child with empathy and understanding, she will treat others the same way. Conversely, without empathy, your child won't feel loved, no matter how much you love her.

The Attunetion Approach provides the path to building love, accountability, and empathy into your relationship with your child. Here's how:

- **When you pay attention and tune in to the right thing for your child,** when you see your child as a separate person with her own temperament and feelings, you take the first step in understanding who your child is.

- **When you pay attention and tune in to the right thing at the right time,** you can verbalize these observations in such a way that your child feels understood and valued.

- **And when you pay attention and tune in to the right thing, at the right time and in the right way for your child,** you can listen with love and respect to how your child feels, understand his point of view— even if it clashes with yours—and then decide what steps you two may want to take next.

For example, let's say your twelve-year-old decides to use your power drill without asking and then leaves it outside in the rain, where it becomes damaged. The Attunetion Approach provides three simple steps to help you pay attention and tune in to the following:

- **The right thing:** You can applaud your child's creative plan to build a tree fort.

- **At the right time:** You can listen to your child and acknowledge his frustration that you weren't home when he wanted to borrow your drill. Accepting his feelings and reflecting them doesn't mean you agree with them, however. You are simply showing him you understand.

- **In the right way:** Rather than arguing or yelling about the broken drill, set expectations and hold your child to them. In this instance, it might mean encouraging your child to take responsibility for taking your drill without your permission and then leaving it outside in the rain. It also means coming up with a way to make the situation right. The goal is to get him to think about solutions himself, not to solve the problem for him. This will enable him to develop a sense of empathy for how you feel and to take responsibility for his actions without excessive guilt or shame.

Right thing, right time, right way: when children feel your Attunetion, deepening your bond is as easy as 1, 2, 3.

Tuning In

Scientists believe that empathy is controlled by the insula, a structure in the brain that is said to be the wellspring of social emotions, such as love and hate, gratitude and resentment, trust and distrust, pride and humiliation, atonement and guilt.

Making the Connection

To help your children tune in to their feelings and the feelings of others, try adding one of the following to your conversation:

- Sounds like you feel...

- You seem worried about this...

- If I hear you right, you're saying...

- So what you're saying is...

- Let me see if I understand you...

- Everyone feels like that sometimes...

- It's okay. I know you'll work things out...

- I know how you feel; that happened to me once...

- It can be hard when...

Think on This

"There isn't any formula or method. You learn to love by loving—by paying attention and doing what one thereby discovers has to be done."

—Aldous Huxley

Catch and Connect: Holding Kids Accountable

Teaching children to be responsible is an essential part of helping them to develop confidence and healthy self-esteem. But what happens when parents don't hold kids accountable for their choices and behaviors?

Consider this all-too-common example. The Morgans have a rule that everyone needs to clean up their bedrooms on Saturday morning before they leave the house. It's Saturday morning, and ten-year-old Max has been watching TV for two hours already. He checks the clock and realizes he needs to get ready for football practice. He gets his equipment together and waits for his mother to drive him to the field.

"Don't forget, Max, when you get home from practice, you need to clean up your room."

After football practice, Max asks if he can invite a couple of friends over.

"That's fine, but you need to clean up your room the minute they leave."

By the time the friends go, it's five o'clock, and the Morgans need to head out for a family dinner with Grandma. When they return later that evening, Max's room is still a mess, so his mom cleans up while Max plays video games with his sister before bed time. No surprise when, next Saturday, the pattern repeats itself, and Max once again wiggles out of cleaning his room.

What's a healthier way to set rules and enforce them? Catch and Connect.

To Catch, ask yourself: do you stand back and let your children learn from their mistakes, or do you routinely give them a pass? Assuming you follow through with consequences, your kids will realize that their choices have a direct relation to what comes next. In contrast, kids who aren't given the chance to experience the impact of their mistakes fail to learn from them and, more often than not, end up repeating them.

If follow-through is a necessary part of accountability, how do you get started?

To Connect, follow these simple strategies:

- **Start as early as possible.** Even small children can learn responsible behavior. For example, have your child pick up her toys before bed. If she is too young to handle the task on her own, get down on the floor and help. But don't do the job for her. Model responsibility by saying, *"I'll do one then you do one."*

- **Set clear expectations.** If you have a rule that your son needs to clean his room on Saturdays, let your child know it. *"Max, I expect you to pick up your room on Saturday morning before you do anything else."* Then let your child know the consequences for not completing the task. *"If you don't have your room straightened out by ten, you can't go to football."*

- **Encourage responsibility.** Teaching a child to be responsible isn't just about holding him accountable for his mistakes; it also means noticing his success. When your child completes a task, tell him, *"Nice job on your science project. I like the way you took responsibility for your schoolwork."*

Bottom Line: Teaching responsibility comes naturally and easily when kids are held accountable. That's because they learn early on that there is a link between what they do and the consequences of their choices.

Your Turn

Responsibility isn't something that comes naturally to children. It has to be learned, starting at an early age. Assigning chores, setting expectations for schoolwork, providing opportunities for positive risk taking—each of these can go a long way toward helping your child develop into a responsible person. However, the most important thing you can do as a parent is to walk the walk yourself—in other words, to hold yourself accountable for the values you want your children to share.

To explore what this means in your household, consider the following scenarios.

1. Think back to a time when you volunteered to help out on a committee at church or at your child's school. Did your actions match your intentions; in other words, did you regularly go to meetings? If you skipped a meeting, what was your reason?

2. Now think about your child. Let's say your son wants to participate in after-school sports. You make the arrangements. However, after just three sessions, he decides he doesn't like the coach. How would you handle this situation?

3. Aristotle is reported to have said, "We are what we repeatedly do." To be an effective parent, you have to do the right thing over and over again for your child to absorb and take on those values. Think of a time where you led by example. How did your child respond?

4. Now think of an example where your actions as a parent may be sending your child a conflicting message about your values—a "do as I say, not as I do" moment. What can you do better next time to help your child understand that each of us is accountable for the choices we make?

Think on This

"When you experience a negative circumstance
or event, do not dwell on it. Be proactive—
put your attention on what you need to do to
bring the situation to a positive result."

—Rodolfo Costa

Three Little Questions to Inspire Change

To help ensure you're modeling the behavior you want your children to learn, ask yourself:

1. What is your **attitude** (your tone of voice, your body language and facial expressions) telling your child about your intentions?

2. What about your **actions**?

3. How can you hold yourself **accountable** for the outcome?

CHAPTER 4:

Who Says You Can Do It All?

Most parents today feel they're doing a constant juggling act, balancing competing demands of work, family, and life. We live in a high-speed, overloaded, split-focus world, where our attention is constantly divided. We multitask our way through the day in an effort to hurry up, go faster, and do it all.

Come on—you've had moments like this when you're physically in one place but mentally all over the map: taking a peek at your smartphone at the dinner table; checking Facebook in the carpool lane; texting away during your daughter's soccer practice; turning your back on your child at the park to talk with friends or read a magazine.

At what cost?

Turns out, we may not be as good at multitasking as we think. In fact, a group of researchers from Stanford University found that doing more often means doing less. Here's why:

While many people say multitasking makes them more productive, scientists say that heavy multitaskers actually have more trouble tuning out distractions and switching from one task to another than people who prefer to complete one task at a time. What's more, evidence suggests that multitasking can impact cognitive abilities, impair memory, and increase stress.[1]

It appears that the more we try to multitask, the more our performance suffers across the board.

The reason is simple: the brain is a sequential processor. This means that each time you switch tasks, it takes your brain several tenths of a second to shift focus. That may not seem like a lot, but those seconds add up as you switch back and forth between cooking dinner and texting your friends, or answering emails and watching the football game.

But what impact does all this distraction have on our ability to maintain that vital connection with our kids?

While technology provides 24/7 access to information and entertainment, it is far too often at the expense of the people and pursuits that have the most meaning and value in our lives. Yet that connection is the building block of intimacy, wisdom, and genuine empathy. Without it, relationships are bound to falter and disintegrate.

So how can you take back your focus? Pay Attunetion to the people who matter most.

Attunetion has three essential components: for real connection to occur, you need to pay attention to the right thing, at the right time and in the right way. To make Attunetion work, set aside what you're doing, put down the iPad, disengage from the television, turn off your cell phone, and focus on the person you're with.

That doesn't mean paying Attunetion has to be time-consuming or taxing. When you can give your child even a few minutes of undivided attention, he or she will feel the energy and respond in kind. Together, you can strengthen and protect your essential bond of connection.

What does Attunetion look like? As world activist Lynne Twist says, "*What we appreciate, appreciates.*"

Ask yourself: when was the last time you stopped in the middle of what you were doing to sit down with your child, your spouse, or your parent and give them your Attunetion?

- As your teenage son opens up about his fears about going away to college, you realize that this is the power of Attunetion.

- As your five-year-old daughter demonstrates her latest karate moves just for you, you realize that this is the power of Attunetion.

- As your aging mother tells the story of how she and your father met, you realize that this is the power of Attunetion.

- As your partner reflects on how far you've come as a couple and a family, you realize that this is the power of Attunetion.

Pay Attunetion to what's grabbing your attention. Turn off the distractions that undermine your focus. Forget about multitasking—be present and pay Attunetion.

- If you turn away to text, even for a second, you may miss an important moment to connect with your loved one…

- If your mind is elsewhere, you may miss an important moment to connect with your loved one…

- If you fill your time with people and things that distract you from what's important, you may miss an important moment to connect with your loved one…

…and these are moments you can't get back. Pay Attunetion to the right thing, at the right time and in the right way. It's that simple.

Tuning In

Sending or receiving a text takes a driver's eyes from the road for an average of four to six seconds. At fifty-five miles per hour, that's the equivalent of driving the length of an entire football field, blind.

Source: U.S. Department of Transportation, National Highway Traffic Safety Administration

Making the Connection

As a parent, it's up to you to model good habits. When it comes to paying Attunetion to your kids, consider the following:

- Make face-to-face interactions a priority.

- Minimize cell phone use when you're with your children.

- Set aside specific times to check in when you're away from home.

- Turn off the TV for extended periods to build distraction-free time with your family.

Think on This

"Wherever you are, be all there."

—*Jim Rohn*

Catch and Connect: Dealing with Difficult Behavior

Have you experienced a situation similar to the one Paul faces as he tries to get his daughter ready for school?

"Come on, sweetie, get your shoes on. Your bus is coming, and Daddy needs to leave for work."

"NO. I don't wanna."

Paul quickly checks his smartphone and shoves some lunch into a bag.

"Stephanie, don't start. Get your shoes on now. I'm not going to ask you again."

"You can't make me. I want Mommy!!!!"

By the time Paul grabs his daughter's shoes, her jacket, and her bag, Stephanie is on the floor, kicking and screaming.

"Stephanie Jean, stop acting like a baby and get your shoes on NOW. I'm leaving without you!"

"NOOOOOOOOOOOOOOOOOOOOOOOOOOOOOOOOOOO!!!"

Mornings are stressful enough without the added complication of needing to deal with a child in the midst of a meltdown. Before the situation unravels further, Catch and Connect.

To Catch, ask yourself why your child is refusing to get ready. Unreasonable behavior may seem like defiance, but it typically means something else is going on—and this something is usually a child who is experiencing fear or anxiety.

To Connect, take a moment to understand what your child is feeling. Put down your smartphone, your briefcase, your child's backpack, or whatever you're cramming into your arms, and pay Attunetion to the right thing, at the right time and in the right way for your child.

"Stephie, I understand it's hard to say goodbye, but I'm going to wait with you 'til the bus comes, and then you have to go to school and Daddy has to go to work. And when school is over, Mommy will be there to pick you up, so let's get ready."

Bottom Line: Recognize that difficult behavior is often a signal of fear or anxiety. Be loving but firm. You want your child to feel that her needs are being met without allowing her to manipulate the situation.

Your Turn

Most parents have high expectations for their children. But when kids encounter challenges, either because of behavioral or learning issues, it's easy to start playing the "blame" game by pointing the finger at someone else. Why is this dangerous? When we make excuses for our children's behavior, we're essentially saying that we see that child as a victim. And when you see your child as a victim, eventually he will see himself that way too.

> *"It's not my fault that I don't have my homework. My mom forgot to put it in my backpack."*

> *"It's Sally's fault I hit her. She hit me first."*

The other problem with the blame game is that it robs children of the chance to learn how to manage themselves and their own lives. They come to believe the rules don't apply to them. And children who don't follow the rules often don't develop and grow into productive, well-adjusted young adults. Pay Attunetion and consider whether you're letting your children off the hook by not holding them accountable for their attitudes and actions by considering the following:

1. Think about any frustrations you have with your children. Maybe it's something simple, like getting push-back on chores or schoolwork. Or maybe it's something more challenging like breaking curfew or

behaving disrespectfully at home or school. Pick one issue and focus on it.

2. Ask yourself: In what ways am I enabling this behavior? For example, if your daughter is taking too long to clean her room, do you tell yourself, "She's too young to handle putting her toys away"? Do you blame your son's sports practice schedule for his falling grades? Or do you point the finger at the Internet as the reason why kids are so disengaged these days?

Here's your chance to turn things around. If you've been making excuses for your child's behavior, break the pattern and stop the blame game. Align your actions with your intentions by saying to your child something like:

"Having to constantly remind you to take out the garbage isn't helping the family. From now on, when you don't take out the trash before you go to bed, here's how we'll handle it. You'll have to walk to school in the morning."

"Let's comes up with a better way for you to handle your schoolwork. From now on, when you don't do your assignments, this is what will happen. You won't be allowed to watch TV or play video games until they're done."

"The way you're treating your family isn't working for me. From now on, if I hear you speaking rudely to your brother, you won't be allowed to use your cellphone for the rest of the day."

Think on This

> "Loss of empathy might well be the most enduring and deep-cutting scar of all, the silent blade of an unseen enemy, tearing at our hearts and stealing more than our strength."
>
> —R.A. Salvatore

Three Little Questions to Inspire Change

To help ensure you're modeling the behavior you want your children to learn, ask yourself:

1. What is your **attitude** (your tone of voice, your body language and facial expressions) telling your child about your intentions?

2. What about your **actions**?

3. How can you hold yourself **accountable** for the outcome?

CHAPTER 5:

What's So Social about Social Media?

S ee if you can relate:

TV mom Claire Dunphy is trying to serve her family breakfast, but no one is paying attention. Husband Phil is engrossed in his iPad, son Luke is busy doing battle on his Nintendo DS, and daughters Alex and Haley are texting each other from across the table. Finally, Claire has had enough:

"OK, everybody...gadgets down...NOW. You're all so involved in your little gizmos, nobody is even talking. Families are supposed to talk!"

Haley quickly texts her sister, Alex, "Mom's insane." And with that, everyone returns to their respective screens.

This scene was from an episode of the ABC comedy *Modern Family*, but it just as easily could have happened in any one of the millions of households across the country: family members sitting together in the same room, totally engaged, but just not with each other.

When it comes to the relationship you have with your kids, your mental, emotional, and physical presence is the greatest gift you can give. Yet being present seems to be more difficult today than perhaps at any other time in history.

Today, nearly 60 percent of American families with children have two or more computers, and more than 60 percent of those have either a wired or wireless network to connect to the Internet, according to studies by the Pew Research Center's Internet and American Life Project. A third of all Americans go online from home multiple times a day, nearly twice the number that did so in 2004.

We've come to rely on a host of so-called "time-saving" devices—smartphones, iPads, laptops, and others—yet they do little to help us sanctify time because they themselves demand so much of our attention.

A recent study by the Annenberg Center for the Digital Future[2] found that "over the last decade the amount of time family members in Internet-connected households spent in shared interaction dropped from an average of twenty-six hours a week to eighteen hours. Meanwhile, complaints of being ignored at times by family members using the Internet soared."

We have more and more ways to communicate but less and less to say. Let's face it: technology is transforming our lives—and not always for the better. Gadgets and technologies give us extra opportunities, including the potential to connect and learn. At the same time, we've created a culture that undermines the power of attention.

Wherever you go these days, you see people talking on the phone while driving, texting while sharing dinner with family or friends, checking email in the middle of a movie. Yet it's hard to have a meaningful conversation when we're always checking the screen. Or when we're saying, "Give me a minute while Daddy makes a quick phone call/finishes this email/watches the game..." You fill in the blanks.

We've become a society so accustomed to letting virtual connections interrupt our day that we don't always see the person who is sitting right in front of us. So what's the message we're sending to our kids? Is it that everyone and everything takes priority over their needs?

Sure, smartphones and laptops enable some parents to spend more time at home, but they've also created a world where we're "on call" 24/7. Facebook, Twitter, and email make it easier to stay connected with friends, but they also make it harder to truly get away for some quality time with your family. The problem is, when you're not physically and emotionally available to your children, it can lead them to wonder, *Why don't my parents want to spend time with me?*

It's not surprising that a recent study found that children often feel that their parents pay less attention to them than to their smartphones.[3] What's more, researchers studying how parental use of technology affects children and young adults found that feelings of hurt, jealousy, and competition are widespread. Specifically, kids consistently cited three examples of feeling hurt and not wanting to show it when their parents' attention was distracted away from them by technology at meals, during after-school pickup, and during sporting events.[4]

When we ignore someone rather than relating to him or her as a person, that individual experiences a kind of rejection or rebuff. And the social brain registers that hurt in the same neural zone that responds when we feel physical pain.

As tempting as it may be to blame technology, that's not the answer. Technology has done a lot to enrich our lives and, besides, it's not going away.

What we need is to find a healthier way to live with the many tech and non-tech distractions of daily life. We need to revive those long-forgotten customs known as family meals and conversation. We need to create an oasis of attention where our kids don't come in a distant last after texts, email, Twitter, and everything else. And that means paying Attunetion to the right thing, at the right time and in the right way for our kids.

- **Pay attention to the right thing.** Be honest: are your Facebook friends more interesting than those you have in real life? Has high-speed Internet made you impatient with low-speed kids? Do you sneak a peek at your phone while spending time with your children? If you answered yes to any of these questions, it's time to pay Attunetion to how technology is shaping your life.

  While there are times when it may be necessary to take a phone call at dinnertime or spend a Sunday afternoon working on the computer instead of enjoying family time, habits that put technology first threaten the vital connection you have with your children and set an example for tech use that kids will follow.

- **Pay attention to the right thing at the right time.** Children model their parents' behavior, including their relationships with technology. Try using your own tech behavior as an opportunity to demonstrate the importance of balance. It's okay to say, *"I've been watching too much television tonight; I missed our family time"* or, *"I let myself get too caught up in answering emails. Let's plan to spend tomorrow evening doing something you want to do."* The key is to use the moment to show your children that even adults need to pay Attunetion to how technology is impacting their time and energy.

- **Pay attention to the right thing, at the right time and in the right way.** Involve your children in setting healthier boundaries around technology—for you and them. Some families establish a tech-free time; others set a timer and limit the amount of family time that they each can use for video games, cell phones, and computers. When your phone rings or you receive a text while you're driving, let your child take the message. And, during family time, like meals or game nights, turn off your phones so that you can enjoy a family connection without interruption.

We need to remember that communication with a child is how he or she learns social interaction. There is no technological replacement for that. In fact, studies show that the more involved—the more connected—parents are with their children, the less likely those kids will be to develop depression and risk-taking habits.

If you are with your child and the phone rings, let voice mail get it this time. If your child wants to talk with you, turn off the television, power down the laptop, and be completely there. When you pay Attunetion—when you pay attention and tune in to the right thing, at the right time and in the right way for your child, your child will feel respected and loved.

Making the Connection

So what if you're sitting side by side on the sofa, each one plugged into a different device? So what if you check your smartphone at the dinner table, in the car, and while you're playing with your kids? What's the big deal? You have plenty of time to connect with your kids.

Is that how you want to play it? Really?

Distracted living is teaching your kids a lot about love and connection—and most of it isn't good. Distracted love can leave your kids feeling ignored, resentful, hurt, and unloved, like they're standing on shaky ground.

If your child is in the room, hug her. If your child is sitting next to you, look him in the eyes and ask him how he is—and mean it. If your child is playing in the backseat of the car, ask her what she's doing. When you pay attention and tune in to the right thing, at the right time and in the right way, you give your child the kind of love that lasts through good times and bad.

Tuning In

One More Reason to Limit Screen Time

Researchers in Australia found that six- and seven-year-olds who spent the most time in front of television or computer screens had narrower blood vessels in the backs of their eyes than children who spent less time. Also, children who spent the most time in outdoor sporting activities had wider eye arteries compared to those who participated in outdoor sports the least. In adults, constricted blood vessels in the eyes have been linked to an increased risk of high blood pressure and heart disease.

Source: The American Heart Association, "Arteriosclerosis, Thrombosis and Vascular Biology", April 2011

Think on This

"Your child needs your presence
more than your presents."

—*Jesse Jackson*

Catch and Connect: Navigating a Sea of Change

Technology can be an extremely positive part of life today, but, like everything else, it needs to have its time and place.

"My in-laws bought our twelve-year-old a Kindle Fire for her birthday. On the surface it seemed like the perfect gift for a tween who loves to read. But when I walked past Chloe curled up on the sofa with her Kindle, I snuck a peek. She wasn't reading her assigned book; that kid was totally engrossed in playing Angry Birds and apparently had been for weeks on end."

Parenting is often about compromise—striking the right balance between what your children need and what they want. Nowhere is this truer than when it comes to technology use and kids. Today, as many as half of all kids up to age eight use Internet-connected devices, 7.5 million kids under age thirteen use Facebook, and 30 percent of apps on parents' phones are downloaded by their children.[5] How do we help them learn healthy habits when it comes to integrating technology into their lives? Catch and Connect.

To Catch, recognize that we're parenting in uncharted territory. Being adept at using technology is an important skill our kids will need to be productive, successful members of society. But the job of teaching kids how to use it appropriately can seem overwhelming when oftentimes our children are more skilled at using technology than we are.

Pay Attunetion to the right thing, at the right time and in the right way for your children: don't let the fact that your children may be more tech savvy than you are keep you from doing what you can to make sure your kids use technology safely and responsibly.

To Connect, discuss with your children safe and responsible online use. Remember, your children are able to connect online at home, at school, and at places in between—where adult supervision may not be present. It's important to teach kids to think carefully on their own about what they're saying, doing, and sharing online. Understand how your child's school is using technology in the classroom at each grade level. And set clear limits around tech use. Some parents insist that cell phones are turned off at the dinner table and that laptops, computers, and cell phones are not permitted in bedrooms.

Bottom Line: Whatever rules you make for your family, the goal is to teach kids how to master technology without it mastering them.

Your Turn

As parents, one of the most important things to tune into is: What do our behaviors, attitudes and ways we take accountability teach our children? Child development expert, Joseph Chilton Pearce once said: *"What we are teaches the child more than what we say, so we must be what we want our children to become."*

The following exercise is designed to help you look more closely at what your way of "being" is telling your children. To begin, select a routine activity from your day that involves one or more of your kids—something basic like cooking dinner, helping with homework, driving home from day care or school:

Without judging, answer the following questions about your activity with your kids:

1. Did your mind stay anchored on your kids and their activity or did it wander onto other things?

2. How did your body feel while you were doing this activity? Did you feel tense or relaxed, tired or engaged?

3. What emotions, if any, did you feel while you were doing the activity? Were you impatient or joyful? Bored or excited? Did you find yourself wishing that you were doing something else?

4. How did the activity go? Were your children cooperative or resistant? Did they seem to enjoy the task or resent it?

5. Pretend for a moment, you are one of your children. What did your behavior and attitude teach them about your priorities? What could you do the next time you miss an opportunity to connect with your child to Catch and Connect?

Think on This

"Every word, facial expression, gesture, or action on the part of a parent gives the child some message about self-worth. It is sad that so many parents don't realize what messages they are sending."

—Virginia Satir

Three Little Questions to Inspire Change

To help ensure you're modeling the behavior you want your children to learn, ask yourself:

1. What is your **attitude** (your tone of voice, your body language and facial expressions) telling your child about your intentions?

2. What about your **actions**?

3. How can you hold yourself **accountable** for the outcome?

CHAPTER 6:

Raising Perfect Kids?
Careful What You Wish For

As a culture, we're always looking for perfection. We want the perfect body. The perfect job. The perfect house. The perfect kids.

Perfect kids—what's up with that?

Sure, it would be easier if your children were always well-behaved. If they picked up after themselves. Asked and answered with a respectful "please" and "thank you." Put their dishes in the dishwasher without being asked. Studied hard and got good grades.

But perfect kids? Would you really want them, if you could have them?

Parents have always wanted the best for their children. But lately it seems that this desire comes with increasing pressure to tightly schedule and manage our kids' lives.

American children have eight fewer hours of unstructured playtime after school each week than they did twenty-five years ago, according to research by David Elkind, professor emeritus of child development at Tufts University in Medford, Massachusetts. Playtime at school is also on the decline. According to data from the National Center for Education Statistics, public school students have on average 1.7 hours of recess time each week, and approximately 10 percent have no recess at all.[6]

Childhoods once spent playing kickball, lazing around on Sunday morning, building forts, and playing dress-up have been replaced by Baby Einstein and kiddie yoga, music and language classes, karate and dance lessons, sports and traveling teams, tutors, college prep courses, and so on.

Giving children every opportunity to succeed sounds like a good thing—and it is. However, when we expect perfection from our children, we rob them of important experiences and the chance to learn and grow along the way. As a result, they often miss out when it comes to developing independence, trust, and self-esteem—in other words, some of the very traits that are necessary for an emotionally healthy life.

In fact, children who are driven to perfection often don't feel confident in making decisions without their parents to direct them. They often have difficulty taking a stand on what they think is right, for fear of upsetting someone. Or they may be reluctant to try something new because they might not succeed. In short, they tend to second-guess themselves and their decisions. As a result, they often experience anxiety, a sense of uncertainty, and a feeling that they aren't "good enough."

So how do you create a healthier kind of "perfect" for your family?

Behavioral science has done a great job of helping us to better understand what makes a child succeed in life. Among the various elements of parenting they've studied, one has emerged as a major player, and that's responsiveness—in other words, how well you pay Attunetion to your children and their needs.

It makes sense.

Children whose parents pay attention and tune in to the right thing, at the right time and in the right way, sense that they matter. As a result, they tend to have higher self-esteem, get along better with their peers, be better at resolving conflicts, and adjust more easily to school than children who are not given the same level of healthy attention.

How can you add Attunetion to your parenting? To raise a child who is resilient and will thrive in any situation, consider the following:

- **Pay attention to the right thing.** *"Brush your teeth." "Do your homework." "Get ready for school."* If you find you continually need to remind your child to do what he or she needs to do, consider this: you may be inadvertently teaching a perfectly competent child to believe she isn't capable of doing anything without your help.

  Pay Attunetion to the right thing, and respect your child's autonomy. In other words, focus less on what you can do to make your child's life easier and more on finding ways to encourage him to take responsibility. Recent research about resilient kids finds that children who do well in life are independent and disciplined and have an internal sense of their own efficacy and abilities.[7]

- **Pay attention to the right thing at the right time.** *"I can't do this assignment." "Mrs. Williams is a terrible teacher." "One of the kids in my gym class is mean to me."* As a parent, you do your best to guide your children in a positive direction and to protect them as they grow. When your child is struggling, this also means paying Attunetion so you can tell whether now is the right time to step in or whether it's safe to let your child "sort it out."

  Pay Attunetion to the right thing at the right time. Tune in to what's happening in your child's world so that you can better understand the issues she is dealing with at school, at home, and in her social settings.

  Let your child know you're there to listen, but recognize that sometimes it's good to let a child handle his own problems. Stepping in every time your child misses a homework assignment, has a disagreement with a friend or sibling, or struggles at sports can be counterproductive. You may solve the problem in the short term, but ultimately you could end up undermining your child's confi-

Tuning In

Studies show that putting kids in charge of their own play provides a foundation for their future mental health. Consider these five benefits of unstructured play:

1. It gives children the chance to find and develop their own interests.

2. It helps them learn to make decisions, solve problems, exert self-control, and follow rules.

3. Kids learn to handle their emotions, including anger and fear, during play.

4. It provides an opportunity to make friends and get along with each other as equals.

5. It provides a source of happiness.

Peter Gray, "The Decline of Play and the Rise of Psychopathology in Children and Adolescents," *American Journal of Play* 3, no. 4, 2011

dence, making him feel as if he isn't capable of succeeding on his own.

• **Pay attention to the right thing, at the right time and in the right way.** *"I forgot my homework." "I lost my sneakers." "I don't have my lunch money."* One of the best gifts you can give your child is to pay attention to the right thing, at the right time and in the right way. Very often, that means respecting your child's right to make her own decisions. It also means letting your child "own" her mistakes when she falters.

Your daughter forgot the book she needs to finish her assignment? Rather than jumping in the car to fix the problem, pay Attunetion to what's happening in your child's life. If she is otherwise happy and well-adjusted, encourage her to talk with the teacher and work it out. Your son is complaining that he's not getting enough play time on the team? Rather than making a call to the coach, suggest to your child that he respectfully speak with him to understand why. Then reassure your child that he or she has what it takes to handle the situation. Doing so will empower your child to be a problem-solver and help him become better-equipped for future situations.

When you learn to step back and give your kids some autonomy, you might be surprised at how much they can accomplish. In the process, you'll strengthen that vital sense of connection between you. You also may feel less stressed and less responsible for your children's day-to-day levels of achievement and happiness.

By building deep roots of Attunetion, you can help your children be resilient, strong, and naturally "perfect."

Making the Connection

Five Ways to Raise Perfectly Wonderful Children

1. **Encourage your kids to entertain themselves—without electronics.** Let them learn to play by themselves. Doing so will teach them self-reliance, foster creativity, and give them time for solo pursuits.

2. **Let your children do homework—on their own.** Check for completion but don't correct mistakes. Teachers get better information when children do their own work, and children learn valuable lessons about maintaining focus and taking pride in their work.

3. **Assign chores—that are meaningful.** By expecting your children to help out around the house, you'll teach them the value of self-discipline and encourage responsibility. You'll also help them to recognize that the success of their family depends on everyone's contribution.

4. **Teach them to clean up after themselves—starting with their toys and their clothes.** Show them how to organize and manage their belongings. This will help them appreciate the value of their possessions and foster a sense of personal responsibility and respect.

5. **Give praise—but only when earned.** This will encourage realistic self-assessment and foster perseverance.

Think on This

> "The right way to begin is to pay attention to the young, and make them just as good as possible."
>
> —*Socrates*

Catch and Connect: Raising Confident Kids

In the book, *The Help,* Aibileen (the nanny) says to her charge, Mae Mobley:

"You is kind. You is smart. You is important."

The roots of self-confidence are born or broken in childhood. That's because early experiences shape a child's sense of self. To cultivate healthy confidence in your children, Catch and Connect.

To Catch, pay Attunetion and let your child know that he is important each day, every day. Recognize the enormous power your words and actions have in fostering confidence in your child. Because there is such a strong parallel between how a child feels about himself and how he acts, helping your child build self-confidence is vital to discipline.

To Connect:

- **Be a positive mirror.** Much of a child's self-image comes from how he thinks others perceive him. This is especially true of preschoolers, who learn about themselves from their parents' reactions. When you give your child positive reflections of his strengths, skills, and talents, he learns to think well of himself.

- **Cheer on your child.** Every child needs encouragement to believe in herself and to take risks and grow. Give your child opportunities to demonstrate her special skills. It may be drawing or singing, doing a summersault, or making her own breakfast. Whatever the skill, give your child a chance to shine.

- **Make a play date.** Playing with your child sends a clear message: "You are worth my time. You are a valuable person." Play can help you learn about your child—his temperament and capabilities at each stage of development. It can also help improve a child's behavior by giving him the feeling of importance and accomplishment. And the more interest you show in doing things with your child early on, the more interest your child is likely to have in doing things with you as he grows.

- **Show trust.** One of the most powerful things you can do as a parent is to let your child know you believe in his abilities. For example, when Marco offers to brush the dog, let him. Instead of micromanaging him, say, "I trust you to do a great job." Although this sounds like a small thing, to your son or daughter that vote of confidence is a powerful message that says, "I can do it" and "I am capable."

Bottom Line: A positive approach to parenting is a vital part of raising a healthy, confident child.

Your Turn

Pick one relationship in your family that could be improved. It could be a relationship with a partner, a child, a parent, or a sibling.

Think about what you could do within the next 24 hours that would make a real difference in that relationship and write your ideas below. Your idea could be as simple as letting that person know that they are special, inviting him or her to share an activity with you, bringing up a subject that need discussion, buying a special treat, or forgiving that person.

Choose one idea and commit to doing it right away. Once you've done it, take a moment to reflect and journal on how it felt to Catch and re-Connect with that special person.

Think on This

> "No one cares how much you know, until they know how much you care."
>
> —*Theodore Roosevelt*

Three Little Questions to Inspire Change

To help ensure you're modeling the behavior you want your children to learn, ask yourself:

1. What is your **attitude** (your tone of voice, your body language and facial expressions) telling your child about your intentions?

2. What about your **actions**?

3. How can you hold yourself **accountable** for the outcome?

NOTES

CHAPTER 7:

When "Good" Kids Behave Badly

Parenting is a joyful, exhilarating, rewarding experience. Sometimes, however, parenting is just plain exhausting. The challenge of raising a child and guiding him or her to adulthood is an enormous task—and it's a task that most of us learn as we go.

Setting limits and being in charge of your children is an important part of the job. Kids need to know that they can depend on their parents not only to meet their needs but also to keep them on the right path. They need to know that their parents have the interest and energy to set appropriate standards of behavior and the skills to follow through.

At times, that means knowing when and how to discipline your child. The Attunetion Approach can help you provide reasonable, consistent discipline to your kids. That's because the Attunetion Approach helps you pay attention to the right thing, at the right time and in the right way for you and your children.

What is the **right thing** to pay attention to when it comes to disciplining your children? Think about the following:

- **What are the rules in your house?** Give some thought to your values and expectations. Remember, children need to be accountable for their own behavior in order to learn the self-control necessary to function as healthy, self-disciplined individuals. Discipline means clearly communicating your expectations, rules, and limits, enforcing them, and then providing reasonable consequences when necessary.

- **How old are your kids?** Discipline needs to be age-appropriate and flexible.

- **What are your triggers?** Pay attention to what your kids are doing that really bugs you. Then ask yourself: is your reaction helpful or harmful? In other words, are you responding in a way that will guide your child to better choices and behaviors?

- **Do your kids know what to expect?** Think about how you discipline over time. Are you steady and even in how you set and enforce rules in your house? Consistency is key to producing positive, lasting change and to fostering good parent-child communications.

When is the **right time** to discipline your kids?

- **NOT when you're angry.** If your child breaks a rule or refuses to follow a request, make sure you take time to collect yourself before responding. Remember, if your emotions escalate, so will your child's.

- **When you have your child's attention.** Make sure your child is focused on you and ready to talk about the issue. For a toddler, this means kneeling down and making eye contact. For a teen, this means making eye contact and speaking with your child without distractions, such as cell phones and friends.

- **EVERY TIME!** If you ask your kid to pick up toys every day but you only follow through every once in a while, he won't learn that rule. Children, especially little ones, need lots of repetition to learn. So don't be angry when you have to repeat the same rule over and over— this is how kids internalize that rule. Consistent repetition is the name of the game.

What is the **right way** to discipline your children?

Each family has its own set of rules and expectations (if you don't have house rules, you need to create some). The important thing is for you to be consistent and predictable in how you discipline your children. Here are a few key tips to consider:

- **Follow the "1, 2, 3 rule"** when your child is misbehaving:

    1. Ask him to stop in a calm but assertive voice.

    2. Tell him what to expect if he does not stop.

    3. Let him know what will happen next and then take action, if needed.

For example,

> *"Owen, I want you to stop climbing on the couch right now, please."*

> *"If you do not get off the couch now, I will turn off Sesame Street, and you won't see the rest of the show today."*

> *"Okay, Mommy is turning off Sesame Street now because you did not stop climbing on the couch."*

- **Make consequences Practical, Specific, and Connected** to the behavior you want stopped. Consider these examples:

Let's say you ask your thirteen-year-old to take out the trash after dinner. As he leaves the kitchen, he says something sarcastic and hurtful. Rather than grounding him for a month, be clear about the consequences, and make sure the punishment is something you can monitor and enforce. *"We don't speak to each other that way in our house. Now, hand over your cell phone. You can have it back when you demonstrate that you can speak to all of us respectfully."*

Then, when you and your child have had a chance to calm down, tune in to WHY he has been disrespectful at home. It's important to remember that all kids have bad days and that there can be lots of reasons he's acting out. Is he pushing limits and testing boundaries, as is often the case with young teens? If so, calmly remind him what those limits are. If something else is happening,

Discipline and Punishment—What's the Difference?

Discipline and punishment are not the same.

- Discipline is a proactive approach to parenting. It's about teaching your children acceptable behavior so that they can achieve competence, self-control, self-direction, self-respect, and caring for others.

- In contrast, punishment is reactive. It's about doling out a penalty to inhibit misbehavior. It may be physical (a spank or a slap) or psychological (withdrawal of privileges, isolation from others, or disapproval).

take steps to understand what's going on and why.

- **Notice good behavior.** All children want to feel like they belong and be recognized for their positive contributions to the family. They also tend to repeat the behaviors that get them attention. As a result, try focusing on their good choices rather than their poor ones. This could mean saying something like one of the following:

"Thanks for straightening up your room today. I appreciate it."

"You finished your homework already? Wow! You're working really hard."

"I see you cleaned up after your snack. Thanks for taking care of this."

"My conference call is over now. Thanks for playing quietly while I talked with my boss."

Remember, discipline isn't about criticism and punishment. It's about building a mutually respectful relationship with your children— one that sets a foundation to help them make healthy choices in their lives. It's not easy to raise children. But when it comes to discipline, the Attunetion Approach helps you to pay attention to the right thing, at the right time and in the right way for you and your child.

Making the Connection

You've Lost It...Now What?

Most people today parent in a rush. When we hurry, we often speak or act impulsively. Is this the behavior we want to model for our children?

If you find yourself screaming and threatening your children, STOP before you do or say something you can't take back. By focusing on your own reaction, you can model for them a healthier approach to dealing with emotions and help them see that they don't have to get frustrated or angry whenever things don't go their way.

Think on This

> "Don't worry that children never listen to you; worry that they are always watching you."
>
> —*Robert Fulghum*

Catch and Connect: Setting Healthy Boundaries

Consistency is crucial in making children feel safe and secure. It's also vital in helping them to develop an understanding of boundaries and expectations. So what happens when kids get mixed messages? Consider this example.

"Our four-year-old has developed a love of bad words. My husband thinks it's funny, but I don't. I go ballistic when I hear Jesse using foul language, but yelling doesn't seem to help either."

No parent would ever intentionally reward bad behavior, but often it happens that way. Sometimes children misbehave just to get attention, even when the attention is negative. To understand why, first Catch and then Connect.

To Catch, pay Attunetion to the right thing, at the right time and in the right way. In other words, tune in to what happens when your child misbehaves. For example, if you laugh each time your child says a bad word, you can be sure your child is going to keep doing it. That's because laughing simply reinforces the bad behavior. The same goes for when you yell and scream.

Rather than playing into bad behavior, Connect for a healthier approach.

- **First, discuss the rules with your spouse.** Have a private conversation and brainstorm ways you can respond consistently as parents when your child misbehaves. Agree on clear, age-appropriate consequences should he continue to use bad words.

- **Second, explain the rules to your child.** Have a conversation with your son and let him know what will happen should he continue to disobey your rules.

- **Third, expect a test.** Behavior doesn't typically change overnight. You may have to reinforce the rules a few times before your child stops the behavior. Whatever happens, don't lose your cool. Instead, tell your son in a calm voice, *"We don't use words like that in our house,"* and then put your plan into action. Your child will stop misbehaving when he realizes that he no longer has an audience.

- **Finally, stay strong.** Do not give in and change the rules. Rather, be consistent and predictable in your response. Children who have consistent rules with predictable consequences are less likely to push the limits and consistently test their parents by misbehaving. They learn quickly that "no" means "no."

Bottom Line: Consistency gives children a sense of security. It also helps them develop a sense of responsibility because they know what their parents expect from them.

Your Turn

Some parents teach their children one thing, but do another. This can be confusing to children and makes for an often dysfunctional home life. Nowhere is this truer than when it comes to expressing emotions, especially anger and frustration.

Think about a time your child was angry or frustrated. How did you deal with the situation? What was the outcome?

Remember, anger is contagious, and often we meet anger or frustration in our kids with anger or frustration of our own. Experts suggest that the best way to teach your child how to deal with negative emotions is to lead by example. Here's how:

To help your kids better manage their emotions, focus on yours first. Think about the last time you felt anger or frustration. What were some of the "early warning" signs that these negative emotions were building?

What strategies do you have for handling frustration or anger in your life? Are you modeling the types of behaviors you want for your kids? If not, what changes can you make to demonstrate a more effective way of dealing with negative emotions?

Now think about your children. What are some of the signs that tell you that your son or daughter is about to lose control?

The more we can help our kids recognize the physical and emotional signs of building emotion, the better they will become at taking a step back and calming themselves down.

While anger is healthy, how we show anger is also important. That's why it's crucial to teach kids healthier ways of dealing with negative emotions. For example, you may want to teach your child to take a break from a difficult situation and step back for a few minutes. During that time, the child can take a deep breath, rethink the situation, and determine what to do next.

List some ideas that you'd like to try with your children to help you and them better manage emotions.

Think on This

> "...seeing with the eyes of another, listening
> with the ears of another, and feeling
> with the heart of another."
>
> —*Alfred Adler*

Three Little Questions to Inspire Change

To help ensure you're modeling the behavior you want your children to learn, ask yourself:

1. What is your **attitude** (your tone of voice, your body language and facial expressions) telling your child about your intentions?

2. What about your **actions**?

3. How can you hold yourself **accountable** for the outcome?

CHAPTER 8

The Gift of Time: It's All about Connection

Children who receive Attunetion are less likely to act out and far more likely to lead happy and balanced lives than those who do not. Why? Because they know how deeply they are valued.

In fact, paying attention and tuning in to your kids at the right time and in the right way is one of the best investments you can make in their self-esteem, future success, and well-being. That's because spending quality time focused on your children helps encourage positive patterns of behavior, decreases exhausting power struggles, and enriches the lives of every family member. Equally important, it can also help protect your children from making poor choices down the road, especially during the harder teen years.

If you're like many parents today, however, you may be feeling guilty about not having enough "quality" time with your children. It's time to put that notion to rest.

Quality time is defined by development experts as meaningful time parents spend nurturing and teaching their children. But here's what's important to understand: quality time isn't about the clock. It's about connecting with your kids and making the time you have with them count.

The Attunetion Approach can help you create this critical connection. That's because the Attunetion Approach shows you how to pay attention and tune in to the right thing, at the right time and in the right way for you and your children.

What do we mean when we say "pay attention to the RIGHT THING"? Your kids don't always need elaborate activities and long segments of time with you to feel loved. They just need the time with you to matter.

To understand the importance of tuning in to the right thing for your children, consider the following suggestions:

- **Learn to let go.** It can be hard to find time with your kids, especially with all that life demands of you each day. But keep this in mind: the dirty dishes or the yard work will always be there; your children will not. Forget the house and job for a moment, and focus on your kids.

- **Prioritize your "must-dos."** Take an honest look at your household chores. Which items are priorities, and which ones can be set aside for now? Maybe some chores can be done less often or after your kids go to bed. And maybe some can be shared by your entire family. Explain to your kids that by their pitching in to help with the laundry or by straightening up the family room, you'll have more time with them to do what they want. You'll likely find that your kids understand the need to prioritize and will be more than willing to help.

- **Make having fun together part of your routine.** Agree to make Friday night pizza-and-game night. Decide that Sunday brunch is time for family only. Sign up to take pottery class with your kids at the Y. Create your own exercise routine, and get your kids dancing and hopping around the house. Whatever the activity, make sure it is age-appropriate and focused on your children.

- **Unplug.** Take a break from technology, and focus on your children. Turn off the cell phones, video games, TV, and laptops, and pay Attunetion to each other. Whether you declare the hour after dinner a "tech-free time zone" or pretend you have a power outage, enjoy unplugged time with your family.

When is the right time to spend quality time with your kids? There are lots of opportunities during the day when it's possible to stop, listen, and connect with your kids. Look for ways to turn everyday moments and errands into special moments.

- **Car Time:** Driving to soccer practice? Take a moment to ask kids about school, sing a song with little ones, or play a car game.

- **Bed Time:** Instead of a nighttime dash through baths and teeth brushing, read a book together as a family or ask everyone what they are excited about for tomorrow.

- **Meal Time:** Eat dinner together as a family MOST weeknights, and talk. During the meal, turn off the phone to ensure uninterrupted time, give each child time to talk about his or her day, and make certain to share something, too. Also, have everyone help in preparing and cleaning up after the meal. Let little ones set the table (just watching them try will be entertaining!), have older ones wash fruits and veggies, and ask your partner to help clear dishes afterward.

What is the right way to spend quality time with your children?

The right way to spend quality time with your kids is whatever makes them feel engaged, attended to, and loved. Here are a few ideas to help you get started:

- Play a board game as a family after dinner.

- In nice weather, take a walk or go to the park together.

- Read books and play with toys with smaller kids.

Tuning In

A recent survey highlighted a disturbing fact: the average parent spends just three and a half minutes A WEEK having meaningful conversation with his or her children. Three and a half minutes— that's all. Not surprisingly, the same A. C. Nielson survey found that when asked which they'd rather do, spend time with their father or watch TV, 54 percent of four- to six-year-olds picked watching TV.[8]

- Go for ice cream or see a movie with older kids.

- Set aside a Saturday afternoon each month for family time, and let a different family member select the activity each time.

To understand the power of the Attunetion Approach, picture this: your whole family is in one place, talking and laughing. You all feel loved and connected. It's not really about what activity you're doing—it's about being together.

THAT'S Quality Time!

Making the Connection

What Quality Time IS	What Quality Time Is NOT
Fostering connection and relationship	Giving technology and other interruptions priority over your child's needs
Giving focused attention	Being distracted while you're with your child
Being attentive, attuned, and responsive	Spending time as a family when everyone is plugged in to his or her own world (iPod, phone, computer, TV)
Saying, "I'm creating time JUST for us."	Squeezing a conversation in with your child as you're racing out the door

Think on This

"When we talk about understanding, surely it takes place only when the mind listens completely—the mind being your heart, your nerves, your ears— when you give your whole attention to it."

—Jiddu Krishnamurti

Catch and Connect: Bonding with Your Kids

Spending time with your children plays a vital role in their development, especially during the teen years. However, teens tend to spend less time with their parents for a variety of reasons, often saying that they want "their space."

"There was a time when Kaitlin told me everything—when she shared what was going on in her life. Now that she's growing up, I hardly see her. She's either with her friends or texting them. She's totally shut me out. I feel silly saying it, but I miss the closeness we used to share."

How do you stay close to your teen, even when your child wants to spend less time with you? Catch and Connect.

To Catch, first recognize that teens need independence to grow up. However, just because your child can do things on his own doesn't mean you should back off from spending time with him. Research shows that when children have close, connected relationships with parents, they are better able to form healthy relationships with other teens and adults. The key is to recognize that your relationship needs to evolve along with your growing child.

To Connect, keep in mind these suggestions for spending time with your kids:

- **Keep it light.** Have fun with your teens, and do things you both enjoy. Don't grill your teen about his behavior and friends each time you're together. Be a good listener; many times teens just want to be heard.

- **Don't wait for your teen to fit you in.** Find time each day to be together and connect. Find activities that easily fit into your schedules—things like making dinner once a week, taking a walk, or working on household chores together. But remember: even five or ten minutes is enough time to share a few laughs or touch base on what's happening.

- **Let your child take the lead**. Ask your teen what would be fun to do as a family, and then do it.

- **Take an interest in what your child likes.** That will give you more to talk about when you're together.

- **When your teen asks for your attention, try to give it.** No cell phone, no Blackberry, no distractions.

Bottom Line: Although they may not admit it, teens need and want your Attunetion.

Your Turn

Dr. Anthony P. Witham once said, "Children spell love … T-I-M-E." It's not surprising; as parents, we all know it's important to focus on our kids. But what happens when "life" gets in the way and your kids have to take a back seat to other priorities?

Don't let feelings of guilt or disappointment seep into your family life. Instead, Catch and Connect. Make sure you sit down with your child and explain why you can't spend the time together that you promised. Doing so send a crucial message to your child that he or she matters. When you treat your kids with this level of consideration and respect, chances are they'll treat you and others this way too.

Take a moment and think about five things you can do to keep your kids close when you have to be away or when life gets hectic.

1.

2.

3.

4.

5.

It doesn't take much to let your children know that they're important. Try writing a quick note and dropping it into their backpacks or lunch bags. It's these connections that make your children feel seen and loved.

Think on This

> "Action expresses priorities."
>
> —*Mahatma Gandhi*

Three Little Questions to Inspire Change

To help ensure you're modeling the behavior you want your children to learn, ask yourself:

1. What is your **attitude** (your tone of voice, your body language and facial expressions) telling your child about your intentions?

2. What about your **actions**?

3. How can you hold yourself **accountable** for the outcome?

CHAPTER 9:

Maxed-Out Minds: The Impact of Technology on Growing Kids

The numbers are staggering. Today, the average American child between the ages of eight and eighteen is exposed to more than ten and a half hours of television, video games, computers, and other media each day, according to the Kaiser Family Foundation. Two-thirds of children under six live in homes where the television is on more than half the time. And nearly one-third of students aged fourteen to twenty-one juggle five to eight different media while doing homework.[9]

What's the impact of this on young, growing brains and bodies?

Researchers are finding that there is a direct correlation between the amount of time children spend with technology and their overall health and development. In fact, many believe that too much exposure to technology is contributing to an increase in physical, psychological, and behavioral disorders that pediatricians, psychologists, and researchers are only now beginning to detect and understand. These include sleep deprivation, obesity, depression, anxiety, and bullying behavior.

According to the Centers for Disease Control and Prevention (CDC), one in six (17 percent) American children aged two to nineteen years old is obese, a number that has tripled since 1980. Those children are at a higher risk of developing type-2 diabetes, asthma, heart disease, and a host of other problems, including teasing, bullying, and social discrimination.

Part of the culprit is our sedentary lifestyle. Children now rely on technology for the majority of their entertainment. Not surprisingly, a Stanford University of Medicine study found that elementary kids consume 20 percent of their daily calorie intake while watching television[10]—calories that aren't being burned off while sitting on the sofa.

But expanding waistlines aren't the only problem experts are seeing. Too much time with technology is rewiring our children's brains, impacting their physical and psychological development. It's also affecting their ability to learn and to form lasting relationships.

Teachers and school psychologists around the country are expressing growing concern that today's fast-paced media is having an impact on learning in the classroom. By the time kids enter the third grade and course work becomes more difficult, teachers are reporting a decline in the ability of today's children to organize their work and focus on the task at hand versus third-graders in the past. Not surprisingly, attention deficit hyperactivity disorder (ADHD) diagnoses are on the rise.

Technology is creating other behavioral issues as well. Social media and texting are changing how children learn and cope with a variety of life situations. Online gossip and slander are becoming commonplace, resulting in painful experiences for kids who are victims of cyberbullying and other acts of cruelty.

Equally disturbing is the impact that violence in video games and other media is having on growing kids. While your kids may think shooting, killing, and maiming are just a game, parents should be concerned about the effect they could have on kids' attitudes toward aggression and their capacity for empathy. In fact, last year, the US Supreme Court acknowledged research showing that violent online video games are a "social problem."[11]

A recently released study by Dr. Vincent Matthews and his colleagues at Indiana University found that those students who played violent video games showed less brain activity in the areas of the brain that involve emotions, attention, and inhibition of impulses. And while researchers are unclear as to how long-lasting these changes may be, many child experts are also concerned that violent video-game playing may desensitize a child's ability to empathize with others.

Researchers are also finding that profanity in the media is having a similar effect. A new study in the medical journal *Pediatrics* suggests that "exposure to profanity is associated with acceptance and use of profanity, which in turn influences both physical and relational aggression."[12]

Of course, not all video games are harmful, and there are actually some benefits to allowing your child to play with some of them. Kids who are familiar with gaming tend to catch on more quickly with computers and other forms of technology. Video games can also build sportsmanship, camaraderie, and eye-hand coordination.

So how do you manage your child's technology consumption so that he or she makes smart choices about gaming and other media? Use the Attunetion Approach to tune in to the right thing, at the right time and in the right way for your child.

- **The right thing** means keeping an eye on what your child is watching and doing. For starters, know the ratings of the video games and movies your child is buying or downloading. Whenever possible, you should play the game yourself. Put media in the family room, where you can more readily monitor what he or she is watching.

- **The right thing at the right time** means supervising your child's media consumption, whether video games, television, movies, or Internet use. When you can't watch TV with your child or monitor his video-game use, spot-check to see what he's watching and playing.

Don't hesitate to put limits on technology use. In one study, a majority of teens admitted that their parents do not impose a time limit on the number of hours they're allowed to play video games. It's not surprising that adolescent girls spend an average of five hours a week playing video games while boys average thirteen hours a week.[13]

- **The right thing, at the right time and in the right way** means modeling good habits around technology. Don't use technology as a babysitter. Instead, balance it with other enjoyable activities for your child.

Tuning In

Studies show that teens who play violent video games for extended periods of time tend to be more aggressive, are more prone to confrontation with their teachers, may engage in fights with their peers, and see a decline in school achievements.[14]

Children who live in homes in which parents and other family members spend a lot of time with technology, including TV, tend to spend their time in the same way. Children who live in homes with a healthier balance of "quiet" time away from the television, the computer, and video games also tend to do the same.

Get involved. Watch TV and play games with your child so that you can experience what they're experiencing, answer questions, and talk about what he sees. When parents pay Attunetion to their family's technology use, they can help their children to be safe and healthy media consumers.

Making the Connection

The Entertainment Software Rating Board (ESRB)

The ESRB is a self-regulatory body established in 1994 by the Interactive Digital Software Association to provide ratings for video games.

- **Early Childhood (EC):** Content suitable for children three years and older. The game has no objectionable material.

- **Everyone (E):** Content suitable for persons age six and older. The game may contain minimal violence and some "comic mischief."

- **Teen (T):** Content suitable for persons ages thirteen and older. Content is more violent than (E) rating and contains mild or strong language, and/or suggestive themes.

- **Mature (M):** Content suitable for persons ages seventeen and older. Content definitely has mature sexual themes, intense violence, and strong language.

- **Adults Only (AO):** Content suitable only for adults and may contain graphic sex and/or violence. Adult Only products are not intended for persons under the age of eighteen.

Think on This

> "A little bit of attention can go a long way."
>
> —*Nicholas Kristof*

Catch and Connect: Setting Limits

"My fourteen-year-old son used to spend every free minute with his buddies. Lately, he's glued to the TV, watching one show after the other and refusing to do much of anything else. Should I be concerned?"

It's not unusual for teens to withdraw socially, preferring to be spend time alone, especially as they navigate the often-rough waters of adolescence. But sometimes when a child withdraws from the world, it can suggest that there's something deeper going on. To help your teen unplug and get back into healthier activities, Catch and Connect.

To Catch what's really going on, pay Attunetion to the shift in your child's habits and the reasons behind it. Tune in to the right thing, at the right time and in the right way for your child. Does your child look lethargic? If so, make sure he's getting enough sleep. If he appears to be unusually withdrawn, using TV as an escape from friends and activities, take a closer look at what else could be going on. Kids who withdraw from their usual social activities could be dealing with bullying, depression, or other difficult emotional or psychological challenges that require your attention.

Don't be afraid to Connect. Talk with your child about what's going on. Help him to sort out whatever challenges he's facing, and then set appropriate limits for TV viewing. To guide him toward healthier choices for his free time, consider the following:

- **Make time for one-on-one fun.** Ask your child to join you on a walk in the park, go to a museum, ride bikes, or play tennis; the key is to find new activities that will reenergize and engage your child.

- **Explore new interests.** Identify new activities that might interest your child. Your local library, community college, or YMCA is likely to offer classes geared specifically for teens. Whether your child tries karate, yoga, acting classes, pottery, or poetry, the goal is to provide opportunities to meet other teens with shared interests.

- **Talk about volunteering.** Capitalize on your child's special interests by encouraging him to give back to your community. For example, if he loves animals, help him to contact the local animal shelter or Seeing Eye organization to help out. If he loves sports, perhaps he can help out at the rec center teaching younger kids to play soccer or swim. Doing so will help your child to feel valued and confident in his talents.

- **Be honest about your own TV habits.** How much time are you spending in front of the TV? Your child may be mimicking your own behavior when it comes to using the television as an escape. Think about things you can do to relax—such as reading, getting exercise, or playing a game—that offer a healthier alternative to hours of TV watching.

Bottom Line: Don't be afraid to be the parent your children need. Setting reasonable limits around TV and other technology is an important first step in helping your children learn healthier ways to navigate the sometimes-uncomfortable challenges of being a teen.

Your Turn

As parents, we're models for our kids' technology use. The problem is that most of us aren't aware of how often we allow technology to impact our family time.

How much time do you think you spend each day talking on your cellphone, reading and answering email, texting friends, and checking your social websites each day?

How much of that time is in the presence of your children?

Now try this exercise. For the next week, keep track of when you're checking your email, answering texts, checking your Facebook page, and surfing the internet and log it below or in your journal. Enlist your kids to help you by letting you know how often they see you picking up your smartphone or logging into your laptop when they're around.

At the end of the week, assess how well you're balancing technology and the needs of your children. If you feel you need or want to make an adjustment, Catch and Connect. Ask yourself: what steps can you take to help limit the time you spend using your smartphone, tablet or computer when your kids are around? Write down your ideas below or in your journal.

When you look back on your life, you likely won't be worrying about the emails you didn't write or the updates to social media you didn't make. Instead, you'll be thinking about your family and whether you did all you can to raise happy and healthy kids.

Think on This

> "Vision without action is merely a dream.
> Action without vision just passes the time.
> Vision with action can change the world."
>
> —Joel A. Barker

Three Little Questions to Inspire Change

To help ensure you're modeling the behavior you want your children to learn, ask yourself:

1. What is your **attitude** (your tone of voice, your body language and facial expressions) telling your child about your intentions?

2. What about your **actions**?

3. How can you hold yourself **accountable** for the outcome?

NOTES

CHAPTER 10

Tots and TV

One-third of three-year-olds in America have TVs in their rooms. And nearly 70 percent of children ages six and under live in homes where the TV is on at least half the time, even if no one is watching it.

You might be thinking, *What's the big deal? TV provides a source of distraction for my kids when I need to get other things done around the house.*

Here's the problem:

Research has found that TV can have a negative impact on the young brains of small children. Not surprisingly, the American Academy of Pediatrics recommends that kids under two watch no TV. Consider why:

- The brains of small children need a lot of play, connection, and physical activity to thrive. When your little one is watching TV, think about what he is not doing: playing, talking, running, learning, or connecting with you!

- Watching a lot of TV, especially if there's a TV in your tot's room, can lead to less family time, less conversation, less connection.

- Watching TV under the age of two can lead to sleep problems and delayed speech development.

So what is the **right thing** to pay attention to when it comes to kids and TV?

Become aware of the negative impact TV can have on young kids, and consider a no-TV policy for children under the age of two. If your child is older than two, take an honest look at how much time he or she is spending in front of the television, and consider setting time limits on TV viewing. Finally, think about when and how you use TV to provide "babysitting" for your child.

When is the **right time** to tackle the TV challenge?

If you need to make dinner, answer the phone, or just need five minutes to breathe, consider the following suggestions:

- Ask yourself what can wait until later. (No one likes unloading the dishwasher anyway.)

- To save time and reduce stress, select easy, quick, healthy dinners, and prepare them while kids play or when your partner gets home.

- Have an older sibling play with your baby or toddler while you take a few minutes for yourself in the other room.

- Invest in a playpen, swing, or jumper toy for your baby to play in while you get things done.

- Complete chores and tasks during your child's nap time.

If your baby is fussy or your toddler seems cranky, try the following before you turn on the TV:

- Change the "scenery". Kids get bored staying in one place. Take your little one outside or upstairs to play in a different environment.

- Go for a walk together. Fresh air can do wonders for an unhappy tot.

- Play with your child. This is how kids learn best. Plus, he or she will feel connected to you.

What's the **right way** to manage the TV when it's on? It may not be practical to expect the rest of your family to leave the TV off when your baby or toddler is in the room, but when it's on, think about the following:

- **What your child is watching.** Make sure programs are age-appropriate. This means not letting your three-year-old watch *CSI Miami*. Also, what's okay for your twelve-year-old to watch is probably not alright for your eight-year-old.

- **Watching the show with your kids.** This offers you a chance to monitor what they see, ask questions, and talk to them about what they're viewing. Plus, you're spending time with them.

- **When the show was made.** Kids' shows that were made even just a few years ago tend to be slower, less stimulating, less graphic, and more nurturing, which is better for developing brains.

- **Setting a good example.** Limit your own TV viewing.

No doubt about it, television can be an excellent source of education and entertainment for kids. But remember: too much screen time can have unhealthy side effects. Pay Attunetion to your children's viewing habits.

Tuning In

In the United States, children watch an average of four hours of TV a day—more than double the amount recommended by the American Academy of Pediatrics.[15]

Making the Connection

Mean What You Say, and Say What You Mean.

Distracted parenting often undermines the effectiveness of parents. Why? Because children quickly learn to slip through the gaps in your attention.

They know that when you say, *"Stop that now,"* you don't really mean *now*. So they use your distraction as an opportunity to keep on doing what you asked them to stop. As a result, distracted parenting adds to your frustration, encouraging kids to push the boundaries.

Think on This

"Tell me what you pay attention to and
I will tell you who you are."

—*Jose Ortega y Gasset*

Catch and Connect: Getting a Good Night's Sleep

For many, TV is a sleep aid—a way to relax and unwind before bed after a hectic day. But what about the impact of TV-watching on kids? Consider this mom's experience:

"My little one loves to watch cartoons with his older brother before bed time. But lately I've noticed something: while my nine-year-old heads right to sleep when I come upstairs to tell them 'lights out,' the five-year-old seems to have a lot of trouble settling down. And he seems to have a lot more nightmares. What's that about?"

If your younger son is having trouble sleeping, it's time to Catch and Connect.

To Catch, pay Attunetion and tune in to what your kids are watching. A new study published in the journal *Pediatrics*[16] finds that watching violent or age-inappropriate programming on TV, in movies, or on computers can increase the odds that young children will have problems falling asleep and staying asleep, or having nightmares.

Many parents assume that cartoons are fine for younger children, but that depends on the content of the cartoon, according to the study's authors. "An 8-year-old can watch superheroes and understand that it's not what happens in real life," said researcher Michelle Garrison. "But that same content can be overwhelming and scary for a 3-year-old."

To Connect your kids to healthier media habits, consider the following suggestions:

- **Watch TV through your children's eyes.** Seemingly harmless cartoons like *Bugs Bunny* and *SpongeBob* may be funny for older kids but inappropriate for younger ones. Better media choices for preschoolers include educational, age-appropriate shows like *Curious George*, *Dora the Explorer*, and *Sesame Street*. Researchers found that making a relatively simple switch in what younger children watch can make a big difference in how they sleep.

- **Watch TV together.** If your children are sitting in front of the TV, join them, even if it's only for a few minutes. That will give you the opportunity to assess what they're watching, discuss the content, and help them to process what they're seeing.

- **Find a new way to wind down.** Studies find that watching TV in the hour before bed time can also disrupt children's sleep by "amping up" their brains. Offer alternatives to TV. For example, encourage your kids to wind down before bed time by reading a book together or playing a game.

- **Teach good TV habits.** Limit the number of hours of TV-watching, and keep TVs and Internet connections out of bedrooms.

Bottom Line: Getting a good night's sleep is crucial to your child's well-being. Studies show that insufficient and disrupted sleep can also lead to health problems in children, including obesity, behavioral issues, and poor school performance.

Your Turn

Television can be a source of learning and entertainment. But studies have shown that too much TV can make kids more likely to be obese—and, depending on the content, more aggressive. That's why it's important to set healthy boundaries around technology, including television for your kids. How do you know what to pay attention to when it comes to the amount of TV your kids watch? The following questions can help you Catch and Connect.

First, think about your own TV watching habits. Do you switch on the set the minute you walk in the door? Leave the television on as background "noise?" Sit for hours watching reality TV while working on your laptop or tablet?

Before you can set rules and limits for TV watching, you need to first understand your attitude around television and the role it plays in your life. Remember, when it comes to kids, actions speak louder than words. Take a moment below to jot down when and how much time you generally spend in front of the TV.

Now think about your children. What is an appropriate amount of time for your kids to spend watching TV each day/week? If you're trying to wean your children off of television, try treating TV as a privilege that kids need to earn, rather than a right that they're entitled to. For example, tell them that TV viewing is allowed only after chores and homework are completed.

One way to manage TV watching is to enlist your kids' help in creating a family TV schedule. Let each child choose a show he or she wants to watch during that time slot, so the viewing is fair. Then post the schedule in a visible spot (for example, on the refrigerator) so that everyone know which programs are ok to watch and when. This will help children get used to a schedule and find other activities to do when the TV is turned off. So that you can guide your kids in this project, jot down some basic guidelines below to help you get started.

Think on This

> "The right thing to do and the hard thing to do are usually the same."
>
> —*Steve Maraboli*

Three Little Questions to Inspire Change

To help ensure you're modeling the behavior you want your children to learn, ask yourself:

1. What is your **attitude** (your tone of voice, your body language and facial expressions) telling your child about your intentions?

2. What about your **actions**?

3. How can you hold yourself **accountable** for the outcome?

NOTES

CHAPTER 11

Get Net Wise: Keeping Your Children Safe Online

Has this ever happened to you? "I tried to check my daughter's Internet browser history, but she deleted it." "My teenager denied my Facebook friend request!" "Every time I walk into my son's room, he slams the laptop shut."

Today's kids are growing up with the Internet. The good news is that they are prepared for a world where computer skills aren't an option but a necessity. The bad news is that most kids can run circles around their parents online, which can make it really tough for parents to monitor their kids' online activity.

Many teens feel that their privacy is being invaded when their parents try to monitor their computer and smartphone use, yet young adolescents may not be tuned in to the dangers that exist on the web. Fortunately, there are plenty of things you can do as a parent to monitor your teen's online activity—even if he or she is more Internet savvy than you are.

To help protect your child from identity theft, predators, and bullying online, try the Attunetion Approach, and keep your kids safe online.

What is the **right thing** for you to be paying attention to? Remember, the first step in tackling any parenting issue is to notice what's going on.

- How much time is my child spending online?

- Who is my kid talking with online?

- What websites is he or she visiting?

- What kind of information is my child giving out online?

- When is the **right time** to tackle the issue of online safety?

Just as you wouldn't allow your child to wander alone into unknown territory, you also would not want him or her to interact on the Internet without parental guidance and supervision. That's why the right time to tackle the issue of online safety is each day, every day, by creating a positive atmosphere of sharing.

- **Learn about the Internet.** If you're just starting out, see what your local library, community center, school, or newspaper offers by way of introduction, or ask a tech-savvy friend for help.

- **Buddy up.** If your child knows more than you do about computers, turn the tables by having him teach you a thing or two about the Internet. Ask where he likes to go on the Internet and what he thinks you might enjoy. The more you can get your child to talk about what's good and not so good about his Internet experience, the better.

- **Don't blame the messenger.** If your child shares with you something that happened online, don't overreact or "punish the victim" by taking away Internet privileges or forcing her to cancel out of social networking sites. Doing so could backfire by leading your child to find hidden ways to get online.

- **Stay informed.** Learn about parental controls that can help keep your child safe online and regularly update them.

What is the **right way** to get started?

Your child may know more about operating a computer or cell phone than you do, but that doesn't mean you shouldn't give up supervising your kid's use of technology. You have one thing your teen doesn't—and that's life experience. Use that experience to help your child navigate the often-confusing and sometimes-dangerous online world.

- **Be on the Alert**. Make sure your child always uses privacy settings.

- **Set limits** around how much time and when each day your child can be on the Internet.

- **Keep the computer in view.** Consider having the computer in the kitchen or family room, instead of in your child's bedroom, so you can keep an eye on what he is doing online.

- **Stay on top of your child's computer use.** Go through the browsing history on your family's computer and your child's smartphone regularly to get an idea of what websites she is visiting. Make a list of approved websites that your child can visit at any time; also make a list of sites she is not permitted to visit. You could post the list next to the computer as a reminder to your child.

- **Block inappropriate content and set limits on downloads.** Some families choose to put a password on the computer so that a child can't log on without a parent's permission. You could also consider parental monitoring software.

- **Name names.** Talk with your child about whom he can communicate with online and what kinds of information he can share. Be clear with him about the dangers of talking to strangers and sharing personal information on the Internet.

- Ninety-two percent of parents are deeply concerned that their children share too much information online.[17]

- More than half of teens have given out personal information online to someone they don't know offline, including personal photos or descriptions of themselves.[18]

- Nearly two-thirds of teens report that they know how to hide their online activity from their parents.[18]

Imagine if you were totally "plugged in" to your child's online activity—how much safer would you feel about him being on the web? Keeping your child safe on the Internet means paying attention to the right thing, at the right time, in the right way.

Making the Connection

Be a "gatekeeper" for your family when it comes to Internet use.

Talk to your children about not posting personally identifiable information online. Remind them that the Internet is a public space and that anyone, including college admissions officers, potential employers, and even predators, can see what they're posting online.

Think on This

"The most important thing in communication is to hear what isn't being said."

—*Peter Drucker*

Catch and Connect: Raising Tech-Savvy Kids

Facebook, Twitter, Foursquare, Tumblr, Pinterest—the list of social networking sites keeps on growing. Also on the rise? A new phenomenon called "Facebook depression."

"Our fifteen-year-old is the picture of confidence. She does well at school, plays sports, and has lots of friends. Recently, though, someone posted something mean about her online. Now Maddy doesn't want to go to school. She's afraid everyone is laughing at her. Our usually bubbly teen is now sullen and irritable. She's holed up in her room watching TV and doesn't want to come out. Should I be worried?"

As parents everywhere know all too well, raising kids in today's technologically connected world can be a challenge. So how you do you help your kids manage the ever-increasing presence of social media in their lives? The answer is to Catch and Connect.

To Connect, first understand that peer acceptance is a crucial part of teen development. If online harassment occurs, symptoms of depression may result. Tune in to your child: is he or she exhibiting sadness, anxiety, difficulty sleeping or concentrating, a drop in grades, and/or a loss of appetite? If so, contact your pediatrician for a consultation.

If your child is otherwise happy and healthy, take this opportunity to Correct. In other words, help your child learn how to navigate the pros and cons of life online.

- **Get up to speed.** Learn how to create a profile, "friend" your child, and share your child's online world. Your child may insist on certain "rules" like not posting on her wall, but that's a small price to pay for having insight into her friends and interests. If you use social media as well, share some of your experiences to keep the conversation going.

- **Talk about what's okay and what's not.** Kids are naturally impulsive and may be quick to post comments that they later regret. Discuss with your child that meanness is never okay, neither is gossiping, saying things that are untrue, or posting anything that could be harmful or embarrassing to another. Remind him that there's no such thing as privacy online—every email, text, or instant message (IM) leaves a digital trail, which schools, college admissions officers, and future employers might access.

- **Declare a tech-free zone.** Don't let your child's reliance on social media replace the need for one-on-one interaction. Set reasonable limits for tech use. For example, insist that cell phones are turned off during meals and other family time. Keep TVs out of bedrooms, and require that your children leave their cell phones in the kitchen at bed time. Teens don't get enough sleep as it is, so enabling them to stay up half the night texting isn't helping.

Bottom Line: Just as you prepare your children for life in the real world, it's equally important to help ensure they're prepared for life online.

Your Turn

A vast majority of parents today feel they don't have the time, energy or computer savvy to know what they're kids are doing online. Yet, the lack of parental supervision of technology sends a dangerous message about our willingness to protect our kids.

For example, the Washington Post reported recently on rise of beauty pageants on Instagram. There, children are judged on their looks based on the number of likes their photo receives. Snapchat, another popular site with tweens and teens, claims that more than 30 million photo and video messages a day are processed as kids upload images of themselves. Because these images are supposedly "gone" once they're viewed, users tend to be bolder in what they send.

However, security experts claim that these screenshots actually last forever and are accessible to anyone with the computer skills to recover them.[19]

How do you know what to pay Attunetion to when it comes to technology? For starters, explore your own feelings about online use and what's appropriate for your children. Ask yourself: what are your attitudes about technology and online access for your kids? Jot them down below. As you review what you've written, consider whether those feelings align with your children's actual use of technology.

How well do you understand privacy settings on various websites? If you're not as computer savvy as you'd like, what can you do to become more educated? Setting ground rules for which websites you allow your children to visit and what information is safe to share is crucial to keeping them safe online.

Think on This

> "...in our never-enough culture, the question isn't so much are you parenting the right way? as it is: are you the adult you want your child to grow up to be?"
>
> —Brene Brown

Three Little Questions to Inspire Change

To help ensure you're modeling the behavior you want your children to learn, ask yourself:

1. What is your **attitude** (your tone of voice, your body language and facial expressions) telling your child about your intentions?

2. What about your **actions**?

3. How can you hold yourself **accountable** for the outcome?

NOTES

The Gift of Being in Attunetion

"**M**ommy? Mommy? Mommy? MOMMY!!!!!!!!!!!!!!!!!"

No one sets out to be distracted. Yet it's very often the people who are closest to us who pull the short stick when it comes to getting our attention. We're with our friends but thinking about other friends. We're out on a date night but preoccupied with our work. We're at a school event but checking email.

No one is really present. In this split-focused world, we gain breadth at the cost of depth and trade in quality for quantity.

Why do we do this?

Is it because we're afraid we'll miss something? The problem is, with so many often-trivial matters dividing our attention, we're missing what's right in front of us.

What would it be like if you gave your children, your partner, your family, your dearest friends the Attunetion they deserve? What if you made a conscious effort to connect to what matters most in your life?

Attunetion is like a muscle—the more you use it, the stronger it grows. The more consciously you pay attention to the right thing, at the right time and in the right way, the deeper your ability to engage and the stronger the foundation you'll have with your children and others.

Years ago, there was a popular bumper sticker that asked, "*Have You Hugged Your Child Today?*" Those stickers are long gone, but the message is more important than ever. We've become so wrapped up in our own lives that we don't pay Attunetion to what matters most—giving our kids the focused attention and nurturing that promote healthy growth and development.

Before you walk in the door from work…before you pick up your kids after school…before you greet your spouse, your partner, your parent, your child… take five quiet moments to **"decompress" from your day.**

- **Pay Attunetion to the right thing,** and remind yourself that the person you're about to greet is more important than any boss, coworker, customer, or acquaintance you've spoken to today.

- **Pay attention to the right thing at the right time.** Put aside your distractions, take a deep breath, and remind yourself that nothing is as precious as the moments you'll have to reconnect with your loved ones. Ask yourself: do the people you love get the experience of your love?

- **Pay attention to the right thing, at the right time and in the right way.** Focus on building that vital connection with your kids. Listen with an open heart to what your children have to say. Notice the twinkle in your son's eyes as he tells you about his big ball game. Feel the pride as your daughter shares her first report card. Let the capacity for Attunetion allow you to truly experience the richness of your life.

Thank you for choosing to read *Parenting without Distraction: The Attunetion Approach* and for your commitment to enhancing your skills as a parent.

Keep in mind that it can take time to transform long-held habits and ways of relating to your family. Take one small step at a time and bear in mind that each time you pay Attunetion, you're one step closer to making your vision a reality. This is your life, and only you can decide what is important and appropriate for you and your children.

Please watch for our Parenting without Distraction journal. It's specifically designed to help you put the Attunetion Approach into action in helping you become the best parent you can be.

Making the Connection

Attunetion is the first and most basic ingredient in any relationship. It is impossible to communicate, much less bond, with someone who can't or won't focus on you.

Tuning In

Whatever you pay attention to—or not—has a huge impact on how you see the world and feel about it. That's because paying attention and listening to your children, even briefly, doesn't just help them; it helps you, too. How? By evoking responses that help you feel cared for, loved, and connected. In this way, Attunetion is like social "cement" that holds families together.

Think on This

> "When your child walks in the room, does your face light up?"
>
> —Toni Morrison

Your Turn

As parents, sometimes we get caught up in the foot race of raising kids in today's split-focus, fast-paced world. But keep in mind, when it comes to our children, it is often the little things, maybe inconsequential at the time, that form the sweetest memories and forge the strongest bonds. They're also the attitudes and actions that speak most loudly about who you are and what you stand for.

So ask yourself: What memories do you hope your children will share with others about you? How will they describe the influence you had on their lives?

Think on This

"Your present circumstances don't determine where you can go, they merely determine where you start."

—Nido Qubein

Three Little Questions to Inspire Change

To help ensure you're modeling the behavior you want your children to learn, ask yourself:

1. What is your **attitude** (your tone of voice, your body language and facial expressions) telling your child about your intentions?

2. What about your **actions**?

3. How can you hold yourself **accountable** for the outcome?

1. Eyal Ophir, Clifford Nass, and Anthony Wagner, "Cognitive Control in Media Multitaskers," *Proceedings of the National Academy of Sciences,* 106, no. 37, September 15, 2009

2. "The Digital Future Project 2011," *USC Annenberg School for Communication and Journalism,* June 2011

3. "AnyBody: Parents Are Ignoring Their Children for Their BlackBerry," *The Washington Post,* January 31, 2011

4. Julie Scelfo, "The Risks of Parenting While Plugged In," *The New York Times,* June 9, 2010

5. Lynette Owens, "5 Ways to Teach Kids to Use Technology Safely," *Washington Post,* July 31, 2012, http://www.washingtonpost.com

6. Mercedes White, "Study Says Kids Today Play Less but Imagine More Than Their Counterparts from 1980s," *Deseret News,* July 23, 2012

7. Dr. Paul J. Donahue, "Why You Should Do Less for Your Kids," *Local Living Magazine,* September 2011, http://www.locallivingmag.com

8. A. C. Nielson Co., "Television Watching Statistics," *BLS American Time Use Survey,* February 7, 2012, http://www.StatisticBrain.com

9. Victoria Rideout, Elizabeth Vanderwater, and Ellen Wartella, "Zero to Six: Electronic Media in the Lives of Infants, Toddlers and Preschoolers", *The Henry J. Kaiser Family Foundation,* 2003.

10. Thomas Robinson, MD, MPH, *Stanford Prevention Research Center,* 2004

11. Tony Dokoupil, "Zombie Apocalypse," *Newsweek,* June 18, 2012

12. Sarah Coyne, "Profanity in TV and Video Games Linked to Teen Aggression," *Science Daily,* October 17, 2011

13. Douglas A. Gentile, Paul Lynch, Jennifer Linder and David Walsh, "The Impact of Video Games on Children", *Palo Alto Medical Foundation*, 2012

14. Douglas A. Gentile and Craig A. Anderson, "Violent Video Games: The Effects on Youth, and Public Policy Implications," *Handbook of Children, Culture, and Violence*, Thousand Oaks, CA: Sage Publishing, 2006

15. *KidsHealth, Nemours,* http://www.KidsHealth/parent/positive/family/tv.org, 2012

16. Michelle M. Garrison, PhD, and Dimitri A. Christakis, MD, MPH, "The Impact of a Health Media Use Intervention on Sleep in Preschool Children," *Pediatrics* 130, no. 3, September 1, 2012

17. *Zogby International,* "Online Privacy: What Does It Mean to Parents and Kids?" *Common Sense Media,* 2010

18. *McAfee/Harris Interactive,* "Moms and Teens Survey", *2009*

19. Kleinberg, Scott. *Chicago Tribune.* "Disconnected, Parents, Kids and the Internet," June 6, 2013.

Made in the USA
Monee, IL
11 March 2021